How to beat the Family Courts

BY
ALEXANDER WILLIAMS

Manhandle Press, England, 2020

How to beat the Family Courts. Edition, 2020, v 1.00.
Published by Manhandle Press Ltd (a company incorporated in England and Wales).

First Published, September, 2020

ISBN: 978-0-9926685-5-6
Editor: M. A. Lindsay MA (Oxon) MBA (Hons) MCIM Cert. Ed.
Cover design by S. Carpenter (www.stephencarpenter.com)
With special thanks to Ian Smith (Peter & Paul Associates) and Paul Apreda for their advice on specific chapters of this book.
Also thanks to JD & J Design (USA) and AT Proof Reading (UK) for their services.

Dedicated to all those who have suffered the "extreme emotional hardship" of the UK Family Courts unnecessarily siding with one parent over the other. In the ironic words of Lord Judge, when sentencing a father to 14 years in prison for removing his son from the UK,

"[Removing]… children from a loving parent is an offence of unspeakable cruelty to the loving parent and to the child or children, whatever they may later think of the parent from whom they have been estranged as a result…" [Tom Whitehead, *Child Abduction*, The Telegraph, 13th December, 2011].

CONTENTS

Foreword

READ THIS FIRST

My intention in writing this book is to help men who just want to be fathers. To this end, I give opinions on how to cope with gender-bias found in the law courts that deal with disputes over children, following the divorce or separation of their parents. As these disputes may involve wider issues I should be clear that I do not discuss: financial disputes, property settlements, Public Law action by social services, divorce proceedings, or anything to do with newly defined parenthood resulting from medical intervention or same-sex marriages. The topic of discussion is 'child arrangements orders' made in the Lower Family Courts of England and Wales. Family Courts in Scotland and Northern Ireland have different practices as well as different laws, especially in Scotland, so in those courts most of this work does not apply.

What I have ended up with is a mongrel of a book that tries to do several things. Firstly, this work can be classified as a self-help guide for Litigants-in-Person (LiP). However, it is different from similar books on the market as I have not been trained in the law. This fact should be a warning as well as a description of what to expect, for although I have checked everything in these pages, things can still be wrong, especially in the use of technical words. The English language is a capricious thing; a phrase that says something exact to a lawyer can have a very different meaning to the average person. Amateur students of law, such as McKenzie Friends, often arrive in a no man's land of not meaning the everyday use of a word but failing to grasp the full exactitude of legal meaning. Complicit as I may be in this deficit, what matters to me is the conveying of concepts. I am not trying to train anyone to be a lawyer.

Read as a self-help guide it may be best to go straight to those chapters that are most suited to your situation.

For those who find themselves in the middle of a court case, and need an explanation of what is going on and what to do, I can suggest chapters that depend on your resources. Men in their first-ever Family Court case, but who can afford to pay for lawyers, should immediately read chapters four to six. While fathers who have no money at all, but nonetheless find themselves in a Family Court case, should read chapter five and then chapters 10 through to 13, to get an overview of what needs to be done.

If you are at the stage of only thinking about taking a dispute over children to a Family Court, then it may be wise to work through the entire of this book. Finally, if you are one of those unfortunate fathers who have an ex determined that you will never see your children again, (and is so far succeeding), to you I have devoted chapter 15, which may help a little.

This work does not seek to replace the other forms of help and support available elsewhere, be it books by lawyers, or help from Father Support Organisations, forums or lobbyists. Also, reading this volume is not the same as getting legal advice, nor does it replace expert assistance in settling disputes about child arrangements following divorce or separation. However, what this book can do for you is provide some glue around all of these different forms of help.

The second function of this work is a commentary on the state of Family Courts in Great Britain at the start of the 21st Century.

People seem to assume that with so much bureaucracy in our everyday lives, with so much of what we do stored on computers, and with so many public archives, not to mention students of history, someone somewhere is recording what is going on. My experience belies this delusion, for although we live in an age of form-filling and paperwork, nearly everything gets binned. Be that by official archives, who chuck away 99 per cent of everything they are given, by the courts, who dispose of court bundles and hearing tapes after five years, or computer records that are scrambled or deleted in a mist of digits untraceable by search engines. On closer inspection you will find that the discipline of history is actually the study of important, not common, people. What this means is if you don't record your history, it will be lost forever.

Loss of information about how the Family Courts work is especially likely, for cases concerning children are held in secret save for those who have vested interests, namely the parties to a case and those who make a good living out of the law. As an ex-McKenzie Friend, paid a stipend, I have been privileged to witness many court cases in which I had no attachment or vested interests. My commentary can therefore be objective and plain, untainted by political correctness or a need to exercise deference to the law or the judiciary.

Many are not so fortunate in their ability to speak freely. Every day, fathers and Father Support Organisations grapple with defending children from the potential harm of courts that favour the will of mothers over children's need for shared-parenting by both parents. Such defenders tread a tightrope with social workers and Judges who have all the latitude and power to take children away from loving fathers. If such defenders openly complained about the judiciary, or Family Law, it would threaten the chances of their present-day cases. What is more, such criticism would hand victory to extremist organisations that have so successfully lobbied for bias, by polarising a war-of-the-sexes in our courts. For this reason I should make it clear that the observations expressed in this book are solely mine. Further, I do not purport to represent any organisation or the views of fathers in general.

While some may be alarmed at what I write, I hope others find illuminating my examination of the politics and intrigues surrounding Family Law and lawmaking, which I touch on in chapters seven to nine. Finally, for those who have been through it all, in chapter 16 I suggest new ways to bring an end to the extremes of injustice I have witnessed, and heard testimony of, for the last 18 years.

Whatever the reason you have come to this volume I can guarantee you a read that doesn't pull its punches in describing the prejudicial machinations and impacts of Family Law on fathers. In my opinion this book is long overdue.

Alexander Williams

1

How do you beat the Family Courts?

In the words of the murdered professor who appears as an interactive hologram in Hollywood's film adaptation of Isaac Asimov's book, *I, Robot*:

"I'm sorry, my responses are limited. You have to ask the right questions."

2

How do you limit the damage of the Family Courts?

"That… is the right question. Programme terminated." [*I, Robot,* 20th Century Fox, 2004]

The law is not what you may think it is. Remember this statement.

The law is not a thing defined by words so much a personal judgment **constrained** by words. In a way, this is an obvious consequence of the law being grounded in the ambiguous media of language. English words, for example, have on average five different meanings. Even a simple word like 'short' can mean a little height, a little length, but also a deficit, or something concise, or about being abrupt. To tighten things up most professions, be they medical, or engineering or the legal profession, invent their own words. Yet, even with special words and phrases for use in a particular profession, language remains deficient. A mathematical formula, diagrams, and physical demonstrations all beat-the-pants-off words in conveying meaning. So it should be hardly surprising that written law is not definitive on its own.

In their origins Judges played a key role in defining law for they represented the will of a King who could not attend every judicial session. A Judge ensured local authorities (or warlords) interpreted the law in writing according to what their King envisioned his words should mean, (or what the King thought of a person regardless of what the hell was written). When this judicial interpretation contradicted the common understanding of words it was the Judge's task to bend logic in explaining the intended meaning.

In reality little has changed in the way Family Court Judges now act, as many fathers find out when they get an order that effectively takes away their children for no obvious reason. The mechanisms of injustice are also much the same today as they were in Medieval Courts, the principal one being: falsely judging evidence.

The image we may have of a modern-day courtroom is of a Judge presiding over a jury who decide a verdict based on facts taken from evidence. Nothing is further from the situation in a Family Court. A Judge makes decisions on his or her own, and there is never a jury. A phrase you often hear in explaining the decisions of these courts is the 'burden of proof'. This is the criteria that must be met by a Judge to accept evidence as being true and reliable. In Criminal Courts this measure is 'beyond all reasonable doubt', benchmarked at 80 per cent certainty. In a Family Court the 'burden of proof' is 51:49. In other words, there only has to be a slightly better possibility of something being true rather than false for it to be found legally true. Equally a Judge can reject an account of events, usually a father's, if the balance of possibilities is tipped even slightly against it. In short, a Judge in a Family Court can decide anything they please about evidence, and there's not a thing you can do about it.

Nowadays, courts do not pronounce the will of a King, and the written word of the law has become very detailed indeed. However, the above Medieval principles survive and shine through. For with latitude given to Family Court Judges a wide variety of judgments could be made on the same type of case. So today, instead of a King, you have Heads of Divisions within a hierarchal court system.

The Head of the Family Division, based in the Royal Courts of Justice in London, sets the interpretation of Family Law through a variety of mechanisms, including Board Meetings of Judges, official memos, and Appeal Court Judgments. High Court cases can also create law, for example, under the process of Inherent Jurisdiction, where a principle is not yet defined in law. Informed in these ways one of the prime duties of a Family Court Judge, no different to a Medieval Judge, is to exercise the intent of the Head of the Family Division.

What you need to be aware of is that the Heads of the Family Courts in the UK, at around the turn of this century, as well as the writers of Family Law Acts (especially the Children Act 1989), have all been feminists. In their time they have wrought a tsunami of change in Private Family Law, to the detriment of the rights of fathers to bring up their children when a separated-mum objects.

This assertion must, or should, seem an outrageous statement to hit you with right at the start. Please don't take my word for it. Sir Mark Potter followed the 'sister act' of Baroness Elizabeth Butler-Sloss, Head of the Family Division from 1st October, 1999, and her co-conspirator in crime, Lady Hale – someone brought up without a father and who helped pen the Children Act 1989. Sir Potter was President of the Family Division and Head of Family Justice for England and Wales from 7th April, 2005, to 5th April, 2010. In a telephone interview on 29th November, 2018, with ex-Fleet Street journalist Neil Lyndon, Sir Potter commented on prejudice in the Family Courts – and here I do ask you to accept his words as the truth:

"The broad approach, the rule of thumb, was that for children up to the age of eight or nine, they would be best off in the care of Mum. After that age, they could largely speak for themselves – though, generally, they would choose to be with Mum. Broadly speaking, the man would be at work during the week, would not be looking after the children during the day, might be doing other things on the weekend and therefore simply would not have been so engaged in the lives of the children.

Continuity of care was extremely important. It would be very unsettling for the children to be constantly shuttling to and fro between two houses, spending half the week at Mum's house and the other half at Dad's. The children needed to know where they were.

The broad consensus of view [of Judges] was, therefore, that care was best provided by Mum. The mother, therefore, held all the cards in the court proceedings. The absolute priority of the courts was to foster the best possible relationships for the child with both parents, but the rulings of the court rebounded badly on fathers. I would have to accept that the dice were all loaded against fathers.

As a feminist, I tend to believe that women are less inclined to behave badly than men, but when you have a mum who is hell-bent on being difficult, it is very difficult indeed to control her. If a mother is refusing contact or doing everything to frustrate it, the court's final sanction is imprisonment – but it is hard to imagine that such a remedy will be in the best interests of the child so it would be highly unlikely to happen."

A potted history of why and how this discrimination in Family Courts was allowed to come into being is doubtless of little primary importance, for if you are reading this book, you are probably a father facing the prospect of losing a meaningful relationship with your children. In the ordinary course of things you will be at a low financially, economically, and certainly in terms of your family relationships. What is more, you may have recently been forced to leave your own home, perhaps with the help of the local police force who escorted you from your property as though a burglar. In whatever way things have come about, you are likely reading this because you are thinking of going to court, or have been through a Family Court process and are wondering where it all went wrong. What you need first of all are answers, not a history lesson.

REVIEWING, THE SITUATION

After years of helping many fathers in the Family Courts my first advice is to give a plaintiff plea, the same as the official position of the Conservative Party. It is also the advice of the Family Courts themselves, namely: **don't go to court!**

The reasons given by the judiciary for this guidance are that the adversarial nature of a court hearing exasperates disputes. Secondly, that these court hearings are an unnecessary drain on the country's trial resources – and the court system cannot cope with the present volume, which nowadays involves some 113,000 children each year, (Private Law applications under the Children Act 1989) (1). The elected Government of the UK has gone so far as to make formal mediation, or MIAM (Mediation, Information and Assessment Meeting), an obligatory first step before any Child Arrangement application is accepted.

My reasons for agreeing with this advice are very different. For if you expect fairness or the proper examination of all aspects of your Child Arrangements application, your expectations are so removed from the reality of Private Family Law litigation that you may find yourself having a nervous breakdown. What these two explanations have in common is a recognition that the processes of the UK's Family Courts are flawed.

But... I have to go to court

To address this statement I need first to throw off the fetters of modern-day political correctness. We are, after all, dealing with disputes between the sexes, of fathers against mothers, a breeding-pair in conflict. As a student of Experimental Psychology I must be allowed to dissect the problem even it means entertaining culturally-unacceptable concepts, no less than Darwin did when he talked about evolution at a time it was blasphemy. I cannot deal with the topic of this book if I have to pussyfoot around 'forbidden words' like 'Newspeak' in Aldous Huxley's *Brave New World* (2). For, despite what we daily see and hear in the media the fact is the genders think and behave differently, especially when it comes to child-rearing. Overlapping Venn diagrams, yes, but there are essential dissimilarities.

The effect of the differences between the sexes is self-evident. Every material thing you are surrounded by, the room you are sitting in, the computer you are using, was probably invented, designed or brought into being by men. Contrary to what feminism would say this is not because women were until recently prevented from creating, building and inventing because of childbearing and men in general. Rather, it is a natural expression of sexual-differences in aspects such as motivation, priorities and attitudes to work.

However, these sex-related characteristics, that serve men so well as builders and architects in human society, can also be a man's undoing in a domestic dispute. For one of the first things fathers want to do is 'sort things out' as soon as they can. This is a male predilection: wanting to tie up with string, put-to-bed, write it down and have it signed off by both parties. For how can you get on with the job of being a single father unless you have rules and schedules? Without them wouldn't it just be chaos and confusion?

In many ways, fathers in Family Court cases can appear Asperger or autistic. They treat their family separation as though running an engineering project or organising a team of men using schedules, rules and memos of work. The sorts of things they want a Judge to decide and force their ex into seeing sense over are just trivia, e.g. timetables, pick-up times, reserving holidays and special days. Much of what men find crucially important in a dispute is simply not – and everyone would avoid a good deal of distress in court if only fathers could be convinced of this fact.

On the other hand, apart from their biological design, women have a unique role in parenting. Within the first months of a new life a biological mother has an irreplaceable connection to an infant's development, something that is intuitively felt and is backed by studies in Experimental Psychology. However, this same science also says that after 18 months a mother is no longer 'all a child needs' – and much trouble in Family Courts would be avoided if only mothers could be convinced of this fact.

My **first tip** is, therefore, dig deep, in whatever way you can and just try to put aside those details in a dispute that could be classed as natural male autism, however much these infuriate you. I mean anything that is not **essential** for the joint rearing of children you love with all your heart. For the truth is, whether or not it was clear to you before, parents stick-it to one another over child-rearing even when they are in love. With babies, it's a game of tag about who is awake to do the nursing, putting down, feeding with a bottle. With toddlers, you can get tagged simply by walking into a room and discovering, as you are about to go out again, that your partner has vanished. So is it any wonder that once love between parents goes, irrecoverably, this sticking-it to one another feels like malice?

I can hear your groans. Putting aside the fine detail, how do you share the upbringing of children with someone you have had an irrecoverable relationship breakdown?

First, let's deal with the negative, which constitutes my **second tip**: if the Family Court is in your head at all, or has been mentioned by your ex-partner, do not write anything down and send it to her. **I mean nothing!** No emails, no letters, no notes, and no voicemail or phone calls (both of which can be transcribed). No social media postings, no photos on Instagram, or anywhere else. Never, ever, go for that killer message that will sort it all out, or sort her out. Only ever discuss things face-to-face, and preferably without witnesses.

At the same time, when it comes to what is sent your way, record, record, record! Keep all letters, emails, social media postings, and start and keep a diary of events. For a father separated from a partner with whom his children still live is vulnerable to misandrist systems of control of his, up until then, private life. At any moment, innocuous details can come under close criticism by those seeking to imply feminist stereotypes. As a consequence, a father in a Family Court case cannot afford to add to this onslaught by using written communication during the run-up to litigation.

I know it is hard to stick to this rule. Over and over again I see otherwise self-confident men resort to writing, texting, or posting on social media rather than face their ex. Yet, these recorded communications typically become the primary evidence in court documents. So regardless of what you may feel, or fear, direct face-to-face contact with the mother of your child or children is the only way to communicate effectively, and the only safe way for an estranged father facing the prospect of court.

Here I need to add a couple of warnings while at the same time encouraging fathers, in the words of a Fathers4Justice slogan, to have a 'brave heart'. You do need to treat encounters with caution. Mothers in child disputes are preyed upon by a plethora of advice, skewed forms, and organisations, all of which entice them to make claims of domestic abuse (CDA). The rewards for such allegations are generous: getting fast-tracked in court processes, a free legal team, as well as having ready-made arguments. Many otherwise honest women give in to this temptation on the basis that 'the ends justify the means'. For these reasons, in any encounter, firstly, keep your distance, no raised voices, and use the salesman's axiom of 'no' said more than twice means no. There are also hotspots to avoid in any meeting-ups, such as school premises, and also any home you have left.

Secondly, this advice **only applies if** there has been no violence, threats or allegations of the same in your past relationship. It does not matter whether these were allegations of violence against you, or the other way around. Approaching someone unwilling to talk to you with whom there is a history of allegations or actual violence, even if you are married to that person, can result in you being arrested. You should also be mindful of the many ways women can then get Injunctions that effectively cut you out of your family without a trial, for example, under the Family Act 1996. In the near future a new Domestic Abuse Law may also give police powers to handout Domestic Abuse Protection Notices, (a replacement of the Police Notice currently used), that will be as powerful as a Family Court Injunction, and could be made permanent after only 24 hours.

The police are directed to pursue all claims of domestic violence without a need for stringent levels of evidence. Also, Magistrates feel empowered by domestic abuse cases and often mistreat alleged offenders. As an example, one of my clients, outside of a Child Arrangement Court case, was given a two-year Non-Molestation Order against him going near or contacting his ex in any way; by phone, in person, or by IT methods. This was because of a Facebook posting he made on his account a year before the complaint. The court passed this order while my client was still in a police cell, represented at the hearing by a solicitor my client had never met, and who arrived 20 minutes late for a hearing that lasted a total of 30 minutes.

Whether because of the threat of false allegations, or because you annoy and tire your ex, the number of opportunities you will have to negotiate face-to-face is limited so you have to make the most of them. With everything in your normal communication-toolbox exhausted you will need some new gears. Most men fail to grasp what it is they lack, which in many instances is an ability to negotiate with someone who has, "All the power." So, my **third tip** is: try assertiveness training before you meet up and go at things in the same old way.

Most fathers I have met say they know how to argue their corner, and they know their ex. Most look askance at any idea of therapy. Yet nowadays, when a domestic dispute is brought into the public domain things can be very different, be it the involvement of the police who automatically side with a mother, or the ease with which women can acquire Injunctions in a culture that accepts women's automatic right to victimhood. New laws make domestic disputes a whole different ball game, and fathers now need new strategies to protect their children. Assertiveness therapy is not about control, but about helping someone to negotiate from a position of weakness and still get what is needed.

An anecdote may give you more food for thought on how else to tackle a difficult ex-partner or wife. Long ago a father-client of mine went through the divorce courts out of which he was given a fair amount of access to his child but was reduced to renting a shared house, and so could not realistically take part in his son's upbringing. By the time the son reached his twenties the relationship with his father was strained. The father experienced long periods of being call-barred, with his son ignoring Fathers' Days and Birthdays. The father knew this was because his child was being fed a constant diet of alienation against him, by his mother and her extended family.

The son then became tragically sick, in a way attributable to the effects of parent alienation, and had some life-changing surgery. One day, after visiting his son in hospital, the father spoke to his wife in one of their rare phone calls during which he broke down uncontrollably in tears saying how much he loved his son and how much he feared for his life. His ex-wife lived with their son's condition day in, day out and so her feelings were more-even compared to the father's, who only saw his son occasionally. From that day on, the son's treatment of his father changed and he now enjoys a more normal relationship.

An answer to some disputes may be found in appealing on different levels such as just saying how much you love your children, **but** without any conditions attached. Not: "I love our children, therefore…" or, "Because I love our children…" or, "Don't forget I love our children…" Just say you love your children, no more. Repeated enough times it may get through whatever is stopping your ex from letting you help raise your kids.

Don't expect any of these suggestions to magically generate a modus operandi for shared-parenting or more acceptable child arrangements. Yet, they could help clear the path. Which brings me to my **fourth tip**: get a qualified mediator or intermediary to write-up what the mother wants, or will agree to, or to edit absolutely essential communication.

We all know that mediation is impossible when one side has all the power, but it can work once some ground is conceded, however small. So however sketchy or inadequate, if contact with your children is offered, despite what I said about not leading with written rules, it is advantageous to have this inscribed (without getting hung up on using the right words or having both of you sign a document). Let me tell you why.

The Family Court Child Arrangement Programme (CAP) advocates unofficial settlements. So if an agreement is made and then breaks down a court is compelled to take such arrangement as the starting point, or status quo, from which both parties must argue for a change. Also, the person who broke the agreement — and surveys find this is normally a mother — will have to explain why they broke it, which puts them on the back foot. So while an unwanted agreement put in writing may feel like a defeat, it can be preferable to the standard situation of a father entering a court case having to justify why things should be changed from a position devised by a mother just before the start of proceedings (such as the father not seeing his kids at all).

However, if it is a father who writes out an agreement it runs the risk of being viewed as coercion. For this reason it is best to use a mediator to draw it up, perhaps as a parenting plan or whatever you like to call it. If you go to the online Family Court Practice Directions 12B, on the Department of Justice website, in section 2.1 there are internet links to mediators (some out of date) in amongst all the other information – **see Appendix IV**.

NB: Many mediators make a good living out of the misery of separated parents and overstate what they do. In my view, MIAMs have become one such scam. Most are done mechanically as non-attendance by one party, a couple of times, will fulfil this requirement – and statistics indicate women are twice as likely to do this as men. What is more, official audits show that only about 12 per cent of MIAMs produce any sort of agreement. The true figure is probably a lot lower as fathers have to get past the widely-held perception by mothers that a court case is: "A faster and more effective way of resolving disputes." (4).

I therefore suggest distinguishing if a mediator is an FM1-form-signing-service, a mediator who does more than just MIAMs, or preferably one that only does genuine mediation.

When it comes to life-or-death, essential communication, get your note edited and signed by either an accredited mediator, or someone like a private social worker, (they do exist). For while written communication is a no-no it is also sometimes unavoidable, so in these instances protect yourself by having what is written professionally checked (and again do not waste your funds on solicitors' letters, they are very poor value for money).

These four tips are basically twofold advice. Firstly, if at all possible negotiate child arrangements face-to-face even if this has failed in the past, and even if this means stopping your ex in the street; but try new ways of talking about things. Secondly, look for new ways to give ground to the mother of your children, to avoid a court case and reach an out-of-court settlement, for the sake of your children.

I am sure my recommendations will receive incredulity. The very last thing on men's minds who are thinking about a Family Court case is rolling over to the demands of their ex, and as for dialogue, "That just ain't going to happen."

I know I am not saying anything new. I know it is common knowledge that not going to court beats a system that we all know is biased against fathers, and you probably have tried every other possible way of sorting things out. All I am suggesting is to give things another go-around, but with a little bit more forethought.

I THINK I BETTER THINK IT OVER AGAIN

For those unconvinced by my tips let me give you some hard facts to help you heed the words of this section's title – as sung by Fagan in the 1960s Musical, *Oliver!* (3). Private Family Court litigation can take three months to get to the first hearing. On average, it can carry on for a total of 10 months, with some cases taking over two-years to complete. The cost of a typical court case, using a full legal team, is between £20–50,000, and for that you get a mere few weeks with a solicitor and a barrister for three or four days. Before spending this sort of money you should consider what you are going up against. Of course, we all differ, but most people view motherhood as something special. Although Judges are supposed to be objective, they are still human, and no less immune to this sentiment.

A natural predisposition for mothers, and a known anti-father prejudice within the Family Courts, brings into sharp focus the adage: you need 'clean hands' to go to court.

None of us are perfect, are we? Everyone has a past which normally includes doing stuff that to a cynic could be called immoral, criminal, or a civil offence. Something minor that we got away with, or maybe didn't? The chances are that if your marriage or partnership has fallen apart, with children involved, something of this ilk may even be in your near past.

I would bet the person who knows chapter and verse on the skeletons-of-your-personal-history is your ex, and for sure she will use them. Such things may seem irrelevant at the outset, — compared to the inhumanity of having your children taken — but they can quickly become the fulcrum on which a Judge pivots a bias judgment. Of course, you may be able to point to faults and failings in your ex as well, but it is not a two-way street, criticising mothers does not have the same effect. What is more, a lawyer cannot protect you from past indiscretions. Solicitors and barristers will not lie about, or hide, facts they believe to be relevant to a case, and if asked to do so they may abandon you (and legally so).

A court case began in haste, starting off being done in your spare time, will, after some months, take over your life, consume your every waking hour and fill your mind. Many men lose their jobs over such action. You also have to take on-board that once you start a case you cannot stop it, only a Judge can. If things start to go against you there is no bailing out, for every application has a counterclaim which means a court case belongs as much to the respondent as it does the applicant. If you do walk away the case could quite happily go on without you.

You should also look closely at what you will end up with, even if you do win, which is merely a piece of paper. That paper can be a potent tool for a mother, but for a father it is different. You can wave the paper around when your ex breaks the order written on it, show it to the police if you like, but I can tell you not a lot is going to happen. Nobody forcibly intervenes with a mother until things have been taken to the very last resort, and no one puts a mother in prison for breaking a Civil Court Order. What is more, and worse, those mothers who are most likely to break Family Court Orders are exactly the ones who know this.

Works cited, but not referenced in the text

1. *Family Court Statistics Quarterly, England and Wales, Annual 2017 October to December.* [S.l. Ministry of Justice, (29th March, 2018)].
2. **Huxley, Aldous.** *Brave New World.* S.l. Random House, 1932.
3. **Reed, Carol.** *Oliver!* Columbia Pictures, 1968.
4. **Hamlyn, Becky; Coleman, Emma; Sefton, Mark.** *Mediation Information and Assessment Meetings and Mediation in private family law disputes. Quantitative research findings.* S.l. Ministry of Justice Analytical Series, 2015.

Making Deals without a Contested Hearing

After separation from a wife or cohabiting partner, fathers can find themselves caught in a triangle of misery. At one corner a father cannot negotiate safely with his ex, face-to-face, because of the threat of protective injunctions, or involvement of the police, or the actual presence of the same. At another corner a father may know that the arrangements his ex proposes, which may be no contact at all, means losing his children forever or risks their long-term development. Such a man may also be well aware of the third corner of misery: that the Family Courts are loaded against fathers.

Caught in this triangle a person can be excused for opting for litigation for at the end of the day the Family Court CAP process, for all its faults, is the only child-arrangement dispute-resolution process a mother **cannot** veto. However, it is also possible for a father to feel he is stuck with only one choice, but still have other options. As there are more choices than a MIAM followed by full-blown Family Law private litigation.

COLLABORATIVE LAW

If you can afford a full legal team for a Family Court case without blinking, (that is around £20–50,000), you may consider that your money is better spent on getting a binding agreement, no different from what you would get from a court, under something called 'collaborative law'.

Collaborative law is a method, rather than a Law Act, based on the way privacy-seeking, wealthy individuals handle, or use to handle, the unpleasant business of divorce. It is about having group meetings, face-to-face, between the parents, with their respective lawyers alongside them, together with whatever experts the couple decide they need including financial advisers, child experts, psychologists and counsellors to get them through sessions.

These 'thrashing out' meetings have an agenda, set by both sides, with the aim of coming to an agreement that can be converted into a draft of a 'consent order' which is then sent to the Family Courts for a Closed Hearing under the Civil Courts Practice Direction 23A (1), (and the parties do not need to attend court although their barristers can). In this process court form C100 is filled in, as per a normal Family Court Child Arrangement application, and sent together with a copy of a signed agreement and drafted consent order. All of this should be handled by solicitors as this process does not work without solicitors on both sides.

Lawyers who take part in such collaborative law meetings can also undertake not to represent their party in a Family Court case should the collaboration not work out – although I fail to see this point written into Resolution's Code of Conduct (the professional organisation behind collaborative law).

The main thrust of collaborative law is financial settlements following divorce or separation, but it does not exclude dealing with child arrangements on their own. It is important to distinguish this method from the normal toing-and-froing of letters between solicitors trying to get an agreement for a consent order. Group face-to-face meetings are the key difference.

FAMILY LAW ARBITRATION

Family Law Arbitration is a different process governed by a different law: the Arbitration Act 1996. In this process you hire a private arbitrator or Judge (sometimes literally as the arbitrator can be a Judge) who decides things for you in a private session, that can be over the phone or in person. Peter Martin, Family Law Arbitrator at OGR Stock Denton Solicitors, said that the arbitration process does not work if both parties are litigants in person, (although he did not rule out the use of a McKenzie Friend on one side), as:

"Solicitors are needed to filter the evidence objectively, as well as to help the parties do such things as getting the safeguarding checks normally done by CAFCASS."

The need for thoroughness in these safeguarding checks is something Sir James Munby emphasises in his guide *Practice Guidance: Children Arbitration in the Family Court* (5), for under the Family Practice Direction 12J a court cannot make a Court Order by consent if there is any doubt about the safety of a child – something that equally applies to collaborative law. Also, for arbitration to be recognised by the Family Courts Sir Munby points out it has to follow the Children Act 1989 for England and Wales. If it follows some other law then the outcome may not be made binding by the UK's Family Courts.

The outcome of arbitration, technically called the 'determination', is converted into a Family Court Order by sending in a C100 form, and when using an IFLA Arbitrator the ARB1CS form, together with the written determination of the arbitrator and a draft of a Consent Order. A Family Court can object to, or change, the detail of this order, but only in the rarest of cases. Case Law from the High Court has set a precedent for this, which reference is: *S v S (Financial Remedies: Arbitral Award)* [2014] EWHC 7 (Fam.), [2014] 1 FLR 1257.

The process of Family Law Arbitration for child disputes is protected by arbitrators being trained by an accrediting body. The big difference over collaborative law is that once a determination is made in arbitration if one party does not like the result there is still the opportunity for the other party to have the decision ratified by an order in the Family Courts, under an 'opposed' process, (whereas in collaborative law mutual consent is needed throughout).

People readily 'get' the idea of collaborative law, but are often confused by what Family Law Arbitration is meant to be. Many mistake it for another version of mediation, which it is not. For while both mediation and collaborative law look to hoick out an agreement that is already there, (albeit buried under a lot of interpersonal angst), arbitration can force a decision that one or both parties do not want in much the same way as can a court of law.

ACCREDITING ORGANISATIONS FOR COLLABORATIVE LAW AND ARBITRATION

Behind the accreditations, for the services of collaborative law and Family Law Arbitration, are a couple of skeleton, membership organisations, whose main substance seems to be their websites. The accreditation body for training lawyers for the collaborative law processes is a private limited company called 'Solicitors Family Law Association' trading as a membership organisation under the name Resolution, address: 91–95 Southwark Bridge Road, Southwark, London, England, SE1. Resolution claim to have 1,200 members as of January, 2019, all of whom have gone through their three-day training course, with a requirement for them to undertake six hours of CPD (Continuous Professional Development) per year to remain accredited.

However, I remain sceptical of Resolution and its members. The sort of thing you see in American movies and TV programmes, with a couple surrounded by their lawyers arguing across a shiny boardroom table, is not what British solicitors naturally do. In reality, with so little guidance a request for collaborative law is likely to degenerate into law firms exchanging letters between themselves. Be warned, solicitors writing to one another is nearly always a sign that your money is being wasted. In my opinion, those who do collaborative law properly are few and are mostly referred from one person to another on recommendation.

The main accreditation and training organisation for arbitrators is the Institute of Family Law Arbitrators (IFLA). This is another incorporated membership company reported to have been set up by Resolution in association with the Centre for Child and Family Law Reform, the Family Law Bar Association, and the Chartered Institute of Arbitrators. The IFLA has no known phone numbers, but only a website — **See Appendix IV** for details — and its address is a PO Box in the Chartered Institute of Arbitrators offices in Bloomsbury Square London, WC1.

Despite the thinness of their organisation an IFLA-accredited arbitrator is a special person, unlike someone with CPD time from Resolution. Although you can source a Family Law Arbitrator from anywhere, (as long as the proper processes are used), an IFLA-listed arbitrator is recognised and trusted by the Family Courts and will ensure a smooth transition from an arbitrated determination, to a Family Court Order.

PROS AND CONS OF FAMILY LAW ARBITRATION & COLLABORATIVE LAW

Collaborative law and Family Law Arbitration have been invented by the Judiciary as new ways of resolving child arrangement disputes. Both processes use existing legal experts — such as solicitors, Judges and barristers — by giving them a few days of accrediting training and then listing them on a website. Both methods are aimed at lightening the work of the Family Courts, although with the same beneficiaries, i.e. lawyers and Judges (complicit in the bad decisions in courts).

In theory, there are advantages to these alternatives to the Family Courts. Firstly, because both arbitration and collaborative law mean you pay for all those involved, (i.e. no free State Judge), and because both parties buy into this expense, it is probable that all parties will behave more rationally. Apart from anything else, both parents are throughout the processes in close proximity to professional people and therefore will be embarrassed at, "Going off on one," (as solicitors are apt to complain).

Secondly, these routes may be cheaper compared to both parties using a full legal team in the Family Courts, funded from the same marital or cohabiting assets. Arbitration, in particular, can come out at half the total cost of two full legal teams – yet, of course, it all depends on the detail of a case.

Thirdly, both arbitration and collaborative law generate a legally binding order **without** the use of the two great evils: a Fact-Finding Hearing or a CAFCASS Section 7 report. Without these instruments, which the Family Courts greatly rely on in making unfair decisions in favour of mothers, a father is simply bound to have a far better agreement – and hang any extra cost.

Fourthly, there is nothing to match the speed of both the above processes compared to the slow meanderings of a Family Court. What is more, in the case of arbitration you can choose your Judge.

The problem with Family Law Arbitration is that it cannot deal with anything involving allegations of domestic abuse or violence. Even if there are no such allegations, but there are other hotly contested facts, a case may be refused for arbitration. Finally, there is no Legal Aid to help with either of these processes — yet both require you to employ a solicitor — and there is no order a Family Court can make to compel anyone to undertake collaborative law or Family Law Arbitration as participation is entirely by mutual consent. However, a Family Law Court case can be adjourned to await the outcome of these processes if the parties do agree to try them.

If either of these dispute resolution routes is of interest then I would advise reading-up in detail about them on the websites for Resolution and the IFLA **(see Appendix IV for the link to the IFLA website)**. To me, the interface between the Family Courts and either a contract/agreement out of collaborative law, or the ARB1CS form in the case of arbitration, seems hazy. I would suggest discussing this topic, along with any others you chose, with prospective solicitors who could undertake these resolution approaches for you. In the case of arbitration, I would insist that it is you (in agreement with your ex) who picks the arbitrator, and not your solicitor, and preferably that you both have a free pre-appointment interview with them.

I should add that in my experience, while both arbitration and collaborative law are laudable ideas they are also, sadly, services without a market. I have seen something like collaborative law used only once, and it was a disaster for the father who had many of his rights and most of his wealth taken away in his desperation to see his children. I have suggested Family Law Arbitration many times, but not once has it been taken up. It seems that either a couple can agree child arrangements after separation, in which case they arrange things themselves or have a solicitor draw up an agreement, (but without the need for collaborative law face-to-face meetings). While other couples cannot agree things, in which case a mother is never going to give-up the advantage of a prejudice court system in her favour for something that is more even-handed.

Yet, we should live in hope. Family Courts are not only unfair to fathers they often create conflict that wasn't there before, and they are truly dreadful places even to visit. If you have the money and an ex-wife or partner that can be convinced to use either of the above alternative dispute resolution methods it will undoubtedly be better for your family.

AGREEMENT ON THE DAY OF THE FIRST HEARING

This option is a bit out of place as it is not something you can plan for so much as an opportunity you can take. The problem with the above methods is that they require you to have ample savings/joint family wealth. Unfortunately, in most cases a lack of money, or opportunity, is exactly what causes family break-ups. Even relatively well-off middle-class couples in Great Britain have little to play with when marital assets are divided in two. In the real world separation or divorce is going to be ruinous for one or both parents, (and usually it's the father).

In the last chapters I deal with preparing for a court case and in those I recommend preparing a backstop position before you make an application to the courts. For with some people being in court can kick-start communication that was until then not offered. It is here, at the doors of the courtroom, that last-minute agreements can be reached before the uncertainty of a case begins. Even though not a single written word is submitted beforehand, if both parties walk into a courtroom with an agreement a Judge will most likely change an initial 'Directions Hearing' into an effective 'Final Hearing' and record that agreement as an order (unless child neglect concerns dominate the case). Family Courts facilitate this type of resolution at the first hearing, not normally in the courtroom itself, but by sending a Cafcass worker to speak with both parties – but be warned this step may be skipped over, so be prepared to make the first move.

However, before those who are being stonewalled by an ex-partner or wife leap at this idea there are a lot of 'ifs'. The first 'if' is if both parties turn up for their first hearing equally manned, meaning with the same provision of legal representation, especially if that representation is zero, i.e. both are litigants in person. If this is the situation, reality can hit home like a debtor facing a claims court.

A father stands a better chance of being offered a last-minute deal if the issues are trivial. Trivial does not mean: where the children will live the majority of the time, or whether a mother can move children away from their erstwhile home town. Details such as whether a child is picked up at 4 or 5 pm, or dropped off at school or the night before at home, fall into the category of what I call trivialities. A lot also depends on the reasonableness of the mother, who ideally should be just tired of talking, but in need of as much help as possible in raising her children.

If such a last-minute agreement is reached it will need to be converted, on-the-spot, into the language of an order. This conversion is best done by a barrister or a very competent McKenzie Friend (see later to find out how these people can be commissioned and what they do). It can also be done by the Judge, but often this introduces misunderstandings.

Be warned, a Judge who agrees with an order drafted by LiPs (Litigants in Person) may alter some of the content, but he or she is not obliged to make a self-devised agreement into a good, sound and legally watertight order in the same way as a barrister. It is, therefore, essential that if no one is legally represented that you ensure key phrases are included in a draft order, perhaps by using a cut-down version of a Final Order template such as a CAP04 – which at the time of going to press was still in use, but you will have to hunt around on the internet to find this template (as its location keeps changing). At the bottom of such an order, use the wording of a Warning Notice to ensure enforceability (if not in the template). An example of this wording is given in Figure 1.

A final point is for those who have a partner teetering on the cusp of sanity at the first hearing; someone who nearly will, but then just won't, agree. While a Judge cannot order anyone to attend mediation, (more's the pity), he or she can adjourn a case to give time for an agreement to be reached, if asked for by both parties. You can then revert to the court to ask your Judge to ratify an out-of-court agreement as a Child Arrangements Order, and this can be done without either party attending court, for example by using email, (if the right words are included and both sign a draft Consent Order).

As a last-gasp attempt to avoid a full court case, if it pleases one party or other, you can try to mollify them by agreeing to an 'Activities Direction' in an Interim Order as a way of facilitating an agreement, (and as long as such intention is written into the order). This normally requires — and at this early stage it would be a voluntary activity — one or both parties attending something such as therapy or some obscure version of mediation, and a lot of the time the mother asks for Anger Therapy for the father. Often, whole court cases that are ostensibly about child arrangements are actually about control, normally control of the father by the mother and her losing that control. Letting the ex have her way may snap-her-back into focusing on the best interests of her children – and I know such Directions can also be a trap to ensnare a partner in a web of lies about alleged abuses. So, I would not agree to any Activity Direction that results in a report, such as psychological analysis – at least not at this stage.

In this last scenario, both parties will likely have to attend court for a subsequent hearing, even if they do then present a signed-off out-of-court agreement, simply so the Judge can hear the outcome of this activity. This route, therefore, runs the risk of allowing the court to force a contested hearing, and a full finding by the court, even if neither party then wants further hearings.

Warning: Where a residence order is in force no person may cause the child to be known by a new surname or remove the child from the United Kingdom without the written consent of every person with parental responsibility for the child or the leave of the court.

However, this does not prevent the removal of the child, for a period of less than one month, by the person in whose favour the Child Arrangements Order is made (section 13(1) and (2) Children Act 1989).

It may be a criminal offence under the Child Abduction Act 1984 to remove the child from the United Kingdom without the leave of the court.

Where a contact order is in force: if you do not comply with this contact order:

a) you may be held in contempt of court and be committed to prison or fined; and/or

b) the Court may make an order requiring you to undertake unpaid work ('an enforcement order') and/or an order that you pay financial compensation.

Figure 1. Example text for a Warning Notice at the end of a Family Court Order.

Works cited, but not referenced in the text

5. **Sir Munby, James.** *Practice Guidance: Children Arbitration in the Family Court.* [Judiciary.gov website. (Online) 26th July, 2018].

4

Tooling Up – Which Trades to Use

"Whenever the warrior draws his sword, he uses it." *Manual of the Warrior of Light*, by Paulo Coelho (6)

Some fathers are just lucky. They fill in a few forms on the dashboard of a white van, turn up to court with a few papers in a plastic bag and their other-half gives in to a mutual agreement at the last minute, which the Judge then signs-off as an order – all over inside of six months.

Many are not as lucky.

If your dispute over child arrangements must go through a full Private Law Family Court process make no mistake, it is going to be a war, and it is foolish to be unprepared. This preparation should at least include reading this book from cover-to-cover, and one or two more besides. Take heed, until you are prepared for battle, or are forced into it, don't talk about the courts. Threatening and sword-waving about what you are going to do, or what you are going to get out of the courts, (when in fact you have no plan, budget or idea of how the courts work), only diminishes you as a father.

A court case can affect your employment if you are in work. You need to forget about holidays for the next year, which you may need to sacrifice for effort in court, and it may be best to advise your employer of what you're doing lest you need extra time off, unpaid. From the start, you need to be sure that you have the time and most importantly enough money, to see what you start through to the end, for once a court case is started you cannot back out of it.

Finally, you cannot go it alone in court and expect to win. Not normally. Not as a father in 21st Century Britain. Whom you should use to help you is all down to your resources, and who you are up against. You should be aware that as a father you can be up against your ex, **and** the court, **and**, typically, social services. Expect all to be your adversaries.

THE BUILDING BLOCKS OF A FAMILY COURT LITIGATION TEAM

The standard reaction of a father faced with suddenly losing his children is either to go straight to a solicitor, or fill in an application to the courts to kick-things-off and then go to a solicitor.

Using a lawyer is somewhat like using a builder. At the start, you may deal with a single person who implies they can do everything for you and will hand-hold you through to the end of the project. However, very shortly you find, after laying down a hefty deposit, this person has subcontracted a lot of his work to people you have never met before, while he becomes more and more unavailable.

Unlike a builder, a lawyer will not even pretend to stick to a quote or estimate, but will run up their bill strictly according to time used. It is therefore worth knowing a bit about the different roles in private law litigation and how they work together and what they cost. For as things go on you may have to chop-and-change whom you use.

There are several different names applied to lawyers: solicitor, barrister, paralegal, legal executive, pupil, trainee solicitor, legal secretary, McKenzie Friend and advocate. The title 'lawyer' is unregulated, so that anyone can call themselves a lawyer, or a legal expert, but it is a crime to call yourself a barrister or solicitor if you are not qualified as such.

Solicitor

You should be aware that solicitors have a special status. They are allowed to handle money for clients, and their involvement in transactions, financial or otherwise, is trusted by the law courts. For this reason, it's hard or impossible to convince a Judge that the other side's solicitors have cheated or lied – and believe me they do both of these things.

A firm of solicitors is a commercial company like any other, but in the form of a Partnership, or Limited Liability Partnership. Owners of law firms are called partners and are usually the founding solicitors who together share the profits of the company in addition to drawing a salary. There are in the order of 9,500 private firms of solicitors in England and Wales, with about 150,000 practising solicitors. In 2018, the number of women solicitors in the UK overtook men as the majority gender, something achieved decades ago in the USA. This change is turning into a stampede as twice as many women as men are now annually accepted to study Law at Universities in Great Britain, and 60 per cent of all early-career solicitors, in 2019, were also female (7). At the same time, in our Universities the vast majority of lecturers for solicitors are also women (with some instructing gender-discriminating subjects such as 'feminism in law'). If a big change in the gender of solicitors is coming it has already arrived in Family Law, with 75 per cent of practising solicitors now female (8).

Solicitors have an unusual way of accounting in that most employees are designated as cost centres. Each employed solicitor, therefore, has a 'recovery rate', meaning the rate at which their time must be charged to recover the costs of their salary, plus overhead, plus profit. This recovery is usually accounted for in units of time, such as every six or eleven minutes. What this means is every piece of work a firm of solicitors does, be it an email, a letter, a phone call, a meeting, travelling to and from the court, is billable in these units. Solicitors keep a detailed note of time in this way; nothing is done for free however friendly a short phone conversation may sound.

In a Family Court case solicitors technically 'conduct litigation', which involves filling in all the court forms, lodging documents at the courts, being the first point of contact for your case, sending and receiving correspondence about the case and liaising with the court on all matters. In other words, they run an expensive secretarial service (and often your phone calls to your solicitor are fielded by a legal secretary to keep your bill down). Unqualified individuals in solicitor firms are referred to collectively as paralegals. Some paralegals may be very experienced and some may be part-qualified lawyers with a degree in Law who could not find a solicitor training post.

Accredited solicitors can speak for a client in some courts, if qualified with 'rights of audience' for that court. In my experience, solicitors do not like doing advocacy work and are not much good at it either. More usually, they will instruct a barrister to do the talking. However, a solicitor who does advocacy could potentially ensure that representations to a

Judge are more mindful of the paperwork, (although solicitors and barristers have a way of working that ensures this transition works most of the time).

Legal Executive

Unlike solicitors, Chartered Legal Executives do not have to have a Law degree and become qualified through vocational on-the-job training and after completing three years of experience doing general work in a law firm. They specialise in a particular area of law, more deeply than a general solicitor, but working in that area is all they can do. Some Family Law Legal Executives are qualified as advocates and can represent clients in the Family Courts. Legal Executives would not normally instruct a barrister, or represent you in the High Court.

Barrister

A barrister, sometimes referred to as a Counsel, is a specialist lawyer (and strangely they do not have to have a Law degree). Their role is to represent a solicitor's client in court through advocacy and negotiation, and to advise the client and solicitor, (together) either in writing or face-to-face, in something called a conference. A trainee barrister is called a pupil.

Barristers are self-employed individuals who work through an intermediary company called a Chamber, to which they pay a commission on all work they receive (something in the order of 20 per cent). Chambers can have many barristers, or be the shell company for a single barrister. The point of contact for Chambers is the clerk.

Most family barristers spend the majority of their working week in court talking in court hearings, whereas solicitors by their nature spend a considerable portion of their week dealing with paperwork. Barristers are supposed to work on a 'taxi rank rule', which means they cannot pick and choose their clients but must take the next piece of work offered, without prejudice. As you can imagine, there are many ways around this rule. In the past barristers did not conduct litigation, and they are not allowed to handle clients' money. However, since January 2014, barristers can now conduct litigation as well.

According to the Bar Standards Board in 2019 there were about 17,000 practising barristers in the UK. Of these, ten per cent were QCs, (Queens Counsels or Silks), being a barrister awarded a higher status, or honour, supposedly based on merit. A 2015 report by the Legal Futures website reported an equal split of genders in this profession, with a slight preference for women pupils.

An advocate in Scotland is a barrister, but otherwise is just a label for a lawyer who does the talking for you in court.

Direct access barrister

Some barristers can be employed directly by you, rather than via a solicitor. Becoming a direct access barrister involves undertaking some extra training. However, even if a barrister is allowed to take work directly with members of the public, not all cases are suitable for this arrangement, especially if there has been no involvement of a solicitor and the case is complicated. If you do manage to get a direct access barrister to represent you at a court hearing, you will need to give them enough notice, usually two weeks as a minimum. You also need to prepare them with copies of the essential papers in your case together with a written 'brief', or explanation.

Apart from the obvious things of appearing on your behalf at court and negotiating on your behalf, a direct access barrister can give advice, such as the formal steps that need to be taken in proceedings in a court. Also, a direct access barrister can draft legal documents and letters if your case goes to court, but these have to be sent in your name unless the barrister is also qualified to conduct litigation. A direct access barrister can also prepare a witness statement for you from what you tell him or her, and can prepare a witness statement from another person based on the information that person provides. If a case requires an expert witness a barrister may advise you on the choice of suitable expert, and draft a letter of instruction for you to send to the expert. Finally, in court, your barrister can draft an order for a Judge, if so asked by the court.

McKenzie Friend

A McKenzie Friend is any person, legally qualified or not, (and nearly all are not), whose activities are formally recognised and described in the publication *Practice Guidance: McKenzie Friends (Civil and Family Courts)*, [Master of the Rolls, Ministry of Justice, 2010]. The idea of this role is to provide support and assistance to a litigant in person (LiP), in or outside a courtroom. In court this might be, for example, by taking notes or finding a particular document, or reminding a LiP of the points they wanted to make but might have forgotten. A McKenzie Friend might also be involved in discussions that you have with the other side's lawyer outside the courtroom, in addition to helping in between hearings.

A McKenzie Friend is not allowed to speak in court unless the Judge makes an exception, and neither are they allowed to directly or indirectly conduct litigation for you. It is permissible in law to share otherwise confidential court documents with a McKenzie Friend, in order to get their advice.

A McKenzie Friend can be somebody you are friends with, or perhaps an extended family member, or can be a paid-for third-party. They must be someone who can understand the situation but who is not so close to the family that they get upset or emotional. It is allowable in law for a McKenzie Friend to charge a fee, but these fees can never be directly recoverable as costs. The vast majority of McKenzies who solicit their services (mainly on the Internet), are men, and are usually fathers who have themselves been through the Family Courts. A LiP must tell the court if they want to use a McKenzie Friend and the respondent in a case is entitled to object to the person you have chosen. Some courts ask McKenzie Friends to provide a CV or fill in a form before letting them into the courtroom.

Private detective

As a father, the burden of proof in a Family Court case usually ends up in your lap. Why? Like it or not, if you say a mother is lying about the best interests of her children, (and nearly all opposed applications do say this) you need substantial evidence to back up these assertions. Having a private investigator (PI) on standby can be a wise move if the contested issues are of the nature of, for example, where and when things are normally done with your children, and by whom. One example of an effective use of a PI was in a case of mine where a mother refused to allow a father to have his son stay all weekend. The mother claimed Saturdays were the most important day of the week with her child as during the rest of the week she worked. The father used a PI to prove that she only worked Saturdays and that she was dropping the child off at a childminder all that day.

There are potential pitfalls in using a PI. They can undermine a father's well-being; for example, lack of findings can bring home how thin a father's argument is for increased parenting-time with his children. A PI may also uncover things a father didn't want to know. A PI may also misunderstand the limitations of evidence needed in court and bring stuff that just character-assassinates the mother, or worse, he may manufacture evidence. The first is not usable and the second is highly criminal.

In general, using a PI also runs the risk of being seen as coercive or divisive. Any clandestine audio or video recordings made by you or a PI are also frowned upon by the courts. However, if the material in such recordings is nevertheless vital to the decision a Judge needs to make in your case these recordings have to be first transcribed into text by a certified transcriber with a statement affirming how the transcription was performed. Finally, the use of a PI could put you in breach of a Protective Injunction, if any are against you. Causing someone to go somewhere or do something you have been legally forbidden to do is treated as going there or doing it yourself.

PIs come from all walks of life, and some are expert scammers and hackers, or others who have supposedly changed the side of the law they work on, so you need to be careful. Try someone who is a member of a reputable association such as the Association of Retired Police Officers. Women PIs can be safer for a father if surveillance is needed.

Child Psychologist

Without pre-empting later chapters, you need to be aware that social workers can be very prejudiced when asked to comment on the thoughts and wishes of a child. There is also an intrinsic vacuum of allowable arguments that fathers can use when seeking more opposed-time with their children. Often the only way to address both of these obstacles is to use a Child Psychologist. However, getting one into a court case is harder than you may think, and the costs more than you can imagine.

You should be aware that while a psychiatrist is a type of doctor, and therefore a professional, a psychologist is not. Anyone can call themselves a psychologist and no one can prevent you from practising as one. However, there are nowadays 'protected titles' that technically cannot be used by just anyone and which are governed by the Health and Care Professions Council (HCPC). 'Child Psychologist' is not a protected title, so what you may instead ask for is a 'Counselling', 'Registered' or 'Practitioner Psychologist', who specialises in child psychology. The other accrediting body for psychologists, that also covers academic psychologists, is the British Psychological Society (BPS), which handles a 'Chartered Psychologist' status. Both HCPC and BPS accreditations are acceptable in the Family Courts. Psychologists are nowadays the most female-dominated job role out of any other in the country. For example, about 98 per cent of Educational Psychologists in the UK are women.

A review by a Child Psychologist should not be confused with a psychiatric review of a father following a Fact-Finding Hearing in which he has been found to have committed violence or domestic abuse. This latter type of review is meant to determine the motive for the facts found, to help a court make decisions at the Final Hearing. Use of a psychologist as an expert cannot be used, as is frequently asked for by fathers, to prove someone mad or deranged, as a Family Court cannot order or direct a person to attend a mental-health examination.

As with any expert in a Family Court case a psychologist is only allowed to contribute when ordered by a court, i.e. unlike all the other roles in this chapter you cannot appoint or use one without the permission of a court. If you ask a court for permission you must be prepared with the name of a particular person, and have their CV ready, as well as an idea of their costs. The appointment of such an expert is done via a letter of instruction, written and agreed by both parties and the court.

Further reading on the subject can be found in *Psychologists as expert witnesses in the Family Courts in England and Wales: Standards, competencies and expectations.* [Family Justice Council and the British Psychological Society, January 2016].

SHOULD I ASK A LAWYER FOR INITIAL ADVICE?

If your ex is using a solicitor, and especially if your case is complicated, seeking legal advice can then be a good step. Whereas, if you are only thinking of starting a court case, but so far have nothing from the other side in writing, a legal expert may not at that time have enough to go on. Of course, you can give your view on what your ex is likely to do and say, but what matters is what is written down and entered into court papers.

There are situations where matters are so serious that seeking initial legal advice is essential, even if you cannot afford these experts for the whole of your court case. These situations might include:

a) Where social services are intending to remove your children or child from home, or where your child has already been removed.
b) When there are allegations of non-accidental injury of a child and the case will include an element of who caused these injuries.
c) When there are allegations of sexual and physical abuse of a child in your care, especially where it is said you are responsible for the abuse.
d) Where there is an international element, such as an application to move a child or children permanently abroad, or where there is the risk of abduction.
e) Where a child was conceived through some form of assisted contraception.
f) Where you do not have parental responsibility.
g) When one party to the proceedings cannot be found, or is avoiding service.
h) When the other party to your application is so mentally unwell they are incapable of handling their case.
i) Where there are more than two parties to the court case.

The benefit of initial advice is that it gives you a clue about what sort of legal team you are going to need to stand the best chance of winning, or minimising your losses. I would set aside at least £600 for a legal opinion on the merits of a course of action in the Family Courts.

You can try, as many do, to circumnavigate this expense. Often this is done by repeated phone calls to different firms of solicitors, each of who give free half-hour consultations, and in doing so give clues and tips on how to run a case. Do this enough times, and you can get the whole initial advice for free. You can then check this with what you have read, and crosscheck with the likes of McKenzie Friends on the phone – many of whom do not charge for talking. However, such an approach is more likely to befuddle than help, and can just leave you stressed and exhausted. If you are finding a decision to go to court difficult, or what sort of applications to make, a full-blown legal opinion may be a wise move as it could save you a lot of trouble further down the litigation highway.

My preferred approach is for an applicant-father to be the architect of his court case. Only then is it sure he will see his case through, and not buckle when the going gets tough. I like to see a father informed about his legal choices and for him to decide on a route using research and common sense, only seeking legal advice if warranted, and then only with a barrister and not a solicitor. But that's just me.

Works cited, but not referenced in the text

6. **Coelho, Paulo.** *Manual of the Warrior of Light.* [S.l. Harper Collins, 2002].
7. *Trends in the solicitors' profession Annual Statistics Report 2017.* [The Law Society, June, 2018].
8. **Hilborne, Nick.** *Family Lawyers 'Disproportionately Female and White?'* [Website: Legal Futures; Posted 2020].

5

Process? What Process?

CHILD ARRANGEMENTS PROGRAMME (CAP) – HEARINGS

Behind the scenes, court processes are manifold and complicated (see Figure 2). Understanding which process applies to your particular case is what legal experts know better than anyone else. However, these professionals are rarely forthcoming without payment, so I give my overview here, for free.

Family Courts handle more than just Private Law Child Arrangement cases. There are property settlements as part of a divorce, and Public Law applications, enforcement applications, injunctions and many other types of hearings. Each type of law case follows its own set of procedural rules. A court case that is about a dispute over how much time children should spend living with each parent, (and under what rules), follows a process defined in the Family Court Practice Direction 12B, known as the Child Arrangements Programme (CAP). You can view these rules online, **see Appendix IV for a link**.

In overview, once you pass some paperwork and mediation steps, the CAP process specifies two or three Preliminary Hearings and then a final, deciding hearing. The Final Hearing can last a few days, and it is here you and your partner sit in a witness box and let-rip, after which a decision is announced and a Court Order is drafted. The two main hearings leading to the Final Hearing are called the FHDRA (First Hearing Dispute Resolution Appointment), the first hearing in a court case, and the DRA (Dispute Resolution Appointment), which is the one before the Final Hearing. If you are unlucky there is another hearing, which **fathers should avoid at all costs: a Fact-Finding Hearing.** This hearing usually sits between the FHDRA and the DRA.

A Judge in court hearings before the final one decides directions, or instructions, on how to prepare for the next hearing. He may give orders that legally require the parties, including social workers and experts, to do things and/or write reports about what they have done or concluded, or to write their account of events or to gather existing written material. All of this can be used to form a formal collection of documents called a 'court bundle'. The contents of this bundle vary in importance, but all of it is meant to help a Judge justify and make a decision.

In truth, maybe only 10 per cent of a court bundle is ever read or digested by anyone. It is very important, therefore, to know the pecking order of all this paper, which is where the skills of a solicitor and barrister can come to the fore (see chapter six for my advice on legal experts).

CHILD ARRANGEMENTS PROGRAMME: FLOWCHART

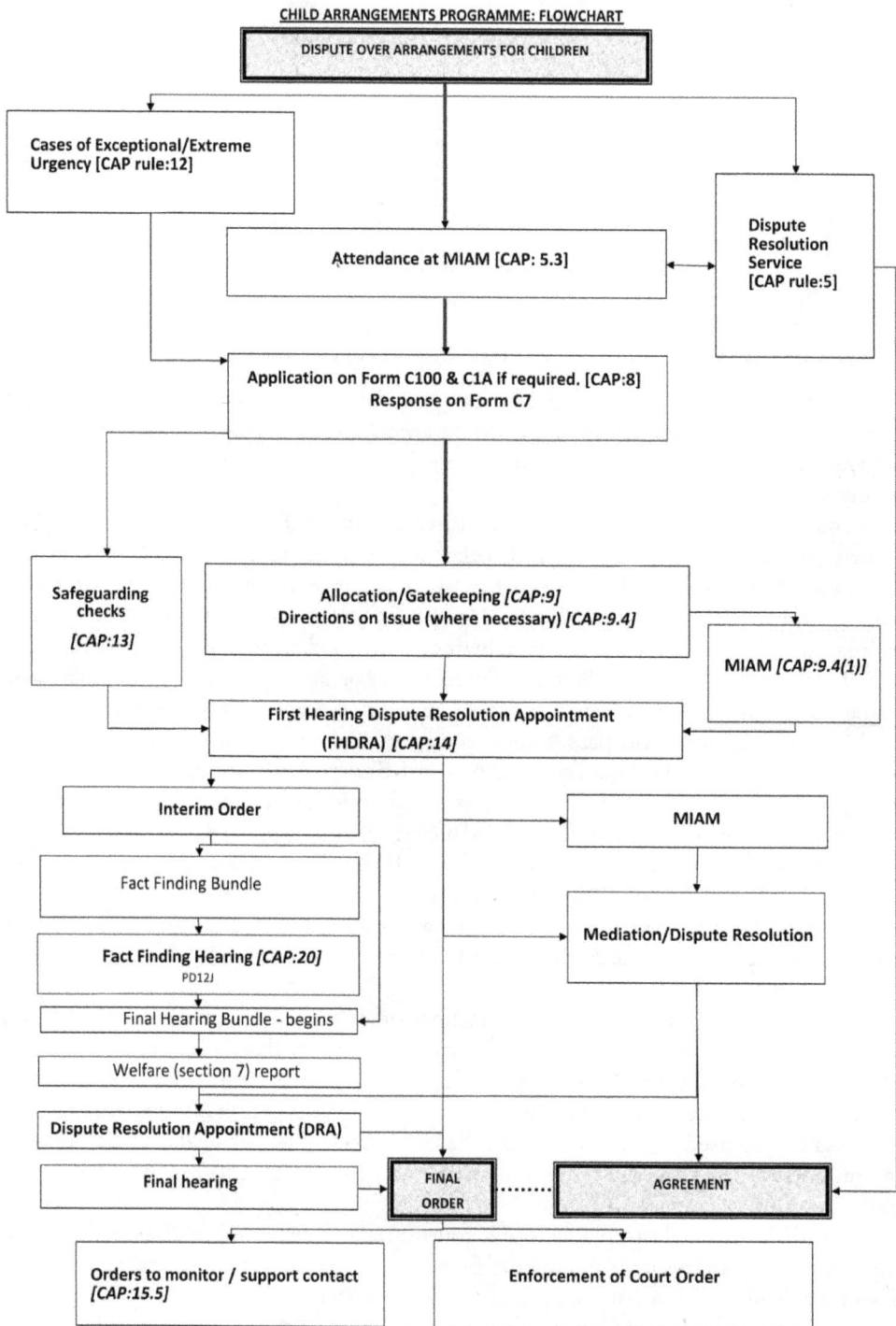

Figure 2. *CAP Court Process as defined by the Ministry of Justice.*

Do not be surprised if different Judges hear different hearings. There is a requirement for consistency, but this is not always able to be met by the courts. An exception is when a Judge 'reserves' all hearings in a case for him/herself, and this is normally stated at the first hearing.

On the whole, I have found that in the South of England Private Family Law Child Arrangement hearings happen in batches. New applications are usually given their first appointment from February to early March of any year, with subsequent hearing(s) around June and an attempt at a Final Hearing towards the end of August. If the opportunity to close a case is missed in August there is usually another attempt at winding things up in October, after which most people have to wait for further hearings in the following year (and usually June of the following year).

THE TWELVE PROCEDURAL-STEPS IN A CAP COURT CASE

These are the steps in the typical child arrangement court case from the point of view of a litigant, as opposed to the point of view of a Court Office as shown in Figure 2, (although the two map onto one another). CAP rules in Figure 2 refer to the section numbers in the Family Court Practice Direction 12B.

What is supposed to happen at each stage and what actually happens, and what criteria are used to go from one step to another, is what has led me to name this chapter *Process? What Process?* In real-life it can be as arbitrary as a driving test of otherwise equally competent drivers. One day one thing happens, and on another, there is quite a different outcome.

1. Start

Taking all measures to avoid a court case is best practice for any court application. Implicit in the CAP process is the requirement for an Applicant to have made reasonable attempts to resolve issues outside of litigation, and these efforts should be documented or detailed somewhere. The CAP process double-checks this requirement by insisting on a MIAM (Mediation Information and Assessment Meeting), prior to submitting an application. However, this does not mean mediation by other means should be skipped over, and the CAP rules list sources of help for people going through a family break-up.

Parents or carers of children are normally able to start proceedings in a Family Court without needing permission. However, in some cases, usually if there has been a previous Family Court case and the Applicant has been given a 91(14) order, (AKA a Barring Order), there is an additional stage to seek 'leave' of the court to apply to start a court case, and this needs to be done on form C2. Even with a barring order in place some applications may still be allowed without the need for permission, for example, if a certain amount of time has passed or if the substance of the application falls outside the scope specified in a Barring Order.

1b. Start with an injunction

Injunction applications are not part of Children Law, nor part of the Child Arrangements Programme. Yet, a lot of Child Arrangement cases now start with, or are preceded by, an injunction application, thanks mostly to the advice given by Women's Support Organisations. Injunctions under the Family Act 1996 are of two types: Non-

Molestation and Occupation Orders (AKA a Go Notice), and should not be confused with Prohibitive Steps Orders under CA 1989. Injunction requests are invariably accompanied by CDAs (Claims of Domestic Abuse) and are meant to prevent an ex-partner or spouse from going near the applicant, and his/her children, or to compel them to leave their marital home.

A temporary injunction can be granted via an ex-party emergency hearing, (without the other party present), if abuse by, or danger of, the other parent is serious and immediate. If a temporary injunction is granted a subsequent hearing is required in which the other party can put their case for not having such orders. Yet, if the accuser in an ex-party injunction then claims an intention to deal with the matter in a CAP court case, this can cause a court to err on the side of caution for them, and on the side of injustice for the accused, by making a temporary injunction permanent. This legal-mechanism has the capability to catapult a Family Court case to stage seven in the CAP process, with only short-hearings had on the way. This way of doing things is, therefore, a neat trick for a mother wanting to have immediate results and load a court case against a spouse, particularly if she is seeking a No Contact Order (and Women's Support Organisations seem to get BBC coverage every time this doesn't work).

2. MIAM [Time delay: two to six weeks]

Before making an application to a Family Court, all applicants for a CAP Order are required to attend a MIAM unless they can claim exemption. Only specially accredited people conduct MIAMs which are very different from marriage counselling or other types of mediation between couples. Exemptions are usually listed on the C100 form in section 19. A typical exemption is if one party is claiming to be a victim of domestic abuse.

If an application presents a situation not suitable for mediation or it cannot progress, for example, because the other party (the Respondent) refuses to attend or acknowledge an offer of a meeting, the mediator signs either an FM1 form or a C100 form, to enable a person to apply to the Family Courts. In this way attendance at MIAMs is not obligatory, and non-attendance does not undermine a party's case. However, a Judge can, even before any hearing is held, refer an applicant back to a MIAM if he/she does not accept the sign-off or the reasons given for being exempt.

3. C100 application [Time delay: decided by the Applicant]

The person who wants the help of a Family Court has to send a C100 form to the Family Court Office and pay the appropriate fee, (or apply for a fee exemption on form EX160). The person making this application is the Applicant.

A C100 application is then assigned to a Judge who starts an internal process called 'signposting', which decides the level of court to deal with the application, the dates of hearings and whether the application is legally acceptable. This process can mean you end up in a court far from where you or your ex lives, and not at the Family Court where you lodged your papers. When a case has an international element, you may find yourself being forced to attend hearings in a High Court, such as are found in the Royal Courts of Justice in Central London. An Applicant should note that a Respondent has the right to ask for a court case to be moved to the nearest court to them.

4. Serving the application [Time delay: if the Applicant is a LiP the Family Court Office will send the application to the Respondent in two to three weeks from a Court Office receiving an application. If the Applicant is using a solicitor it is up to them to serve the application, which has to be done by them at least two weeks before the hearing date]

An Applicant must serve a copy of their C100 on the Respondent, (meaning send it to them) for an application to be valid. Generally, you should not get paranoid about people avoiding service. Most Judges find it hard to believe a Respondent who says something wasn't sent or received if an Applicant says it was, and anyway the court process gives plenty of time for a Respondent to catch up.

An exception may be if a Respondent does not turn up at all. If the location of the Respondent is in doubt, or if the Court Office reports an application is returned, it is **very occasionally** an idea to have the application re-served by a Private Investigator (who can testify that the right person got the application).

NB: Even when an application is served on a Respondent by the Court Office, if the Applicant is a LiP, it is still the Applicant's responsibility to ensure this step is done. So it may be worth a follow-up call to the Court Office and noting when and what was said by the administrators so you can tell a Judge if asked. Court Offices do make mistakes, and these then become the Applicant's mistake. However, the Court Office is **solely** responsible for sending the same application to CAFCASS/CAFCASS Cymru (in Wales) for safety checks to be done.

5. The response [Time delay: two weeks from receipt of application, but four days before hearing]

The other parent named on the Applicant's C100 usually is the Respondent, who should acknowledge receipt of the documents and fill in their answers using form C7, and the form C1A if claiming abuse. It is also possible for a Respondent to make no response to an application, but still take part in court proceedings. An Applicant should receive a copy of the C7 and the C1A at least four days before the first hearing. If the Respondent has no legal representation, this is not a problem as the Court Office will forward these forms to the Applicant. However, if the Respondent is legally represented that lawyer is responsible for sending on these forms. If the Applicant is not represented, but the Respondent is, he can expect to be mucked around over such form sending, and expect the other side to get away with it. As long as the Applicant sees the Respondent's C7 reply at least an hour before a hearing he should not bleat too much about this typical solicitor-trick.

6. Safeguarding checks [Time delay: 17 days from receipt of an application into the Cafcass office, and/or two days before the FHDRA]

Once an application is made it is sent to the organisation CAFCASS, or in Wales CAFCASS Cymru, and in theory, this will trigger them to assign a Cafcass worker, or a WFPO in Wales, to make some safeguarding enquiries about the children named in the application. These enquiries can include discussions with family members. However, social workers are not supposed to discuss the detail of an application at this stage, but only any concerns one parent has regarding the safety of their children whilst in the control of the other parent. Cafcass workers, or WFPO, will also do a screening with the Police, and with Local Authority Social Services, unless social services are already involved with the

Applicant's family, in which case the CAFCASS organisation is supposed to be copied, but take a back seat. If risks to children are identified, or suggested, the Cafcass worker, or WFPO, will do a risk assessment. All of this is entered into a safeguarding letter or report sent to the court for the first hearing.

It is wholly wrong if one party has a copy of this safeguarding letter or report and the other doesn't – and I have seen this done a few times by mother-centric social workers. Such an omission should be cause for a court hearing to be reheard. Do not be surprised if you are not contacted at all, or spoken to only briefly. If a father's children live the majority of their time with the other parent, (pending the outcome of the court case), social workers' attention will primarily be with that parent.

7. FHDRA [Time delay: meant to be five to six weeks, but usually three to six months from application receipt]

The first court hearing is called an FHDRA (First Hearing Dispute Resolution Appointment). All court hearings are supposed to have court bundles, but preliminary hearing bundles are not normally prescribed. The bundle for the FHDRA typically consists of all the forms that have been submitted by both sides to the case and any orders from prior, related hearings. If safeguarding information is not available at this hearing, as it often isn't, the court might make some orders concerning things it considers crucial at that time, rename the hearing as a first directions appointment and postpone the FHDRA. Or, the court may proceed to the next stage despite the lack of information.

Social services nearly always turn up at hearings when they are supposed to, but they are still the primary source of delay in Family Court cases, mostly because of their slowness to produce reports. Courts seem to be powerless to impose discipline on social workers when they fail to do what they are meant to, despite the importance of their contribution. Over the years I have concluded that part of the reason for this slackness is that social workers like to have sight of the statements from all the parties before submitting a report, (and the CAP process does not always give them these when they want). In addition, most Child Arrangement cases start out with children living the majority of their time with their mother. Being a mono-gender institution this situation is always seen as a low risk for children, and so such Private Law cases are not prioritised by social workers. However, every case is different. Sometimes, if the mother's objections to what the father wants are not strongly felt social services can quickly write a report that endorses the father's application, especially if they see that his children are in favour of it.

If, despite it previously being in dispute, everything that an Applicant wants a court to sort out can be magically agreed once in the court building, the Judge is empowered to turn the FHDRA into an 'Effective Final Hearing' and make a Final Order. The court case can then potentially be ended – although sometimes this is a provisional order pending any delayed CAFCASS report/letter which is then read in a subsequent 'closed session'. Only when this second short-hearing is satisfactorily completed, with a Cafcass worker, or WFPO, or the Applicant's family's social worker, can a Judge lawfully close a Family Court case.

7b. Fact-Finding Hearing bundle (if necessary)

If there are disputes about facts that are important to the decision a court has to make about children (usually as a result of a mother playing the domestic-abuse card), about which there is no hard evidence, a court might decide to have a Fact-Finding Hearing. This is an entirely additional, but connected, procedure for which a formal court bundle has to be made. How this document is made should be detailed in Directions given prior to the Fact-Finding Hearing, with a time schedule saying who should prepare what, and by when, and exchange with the other party by when. Often all the detail necessary to get an effective Fact-Finding Hearing bundle cannot be ironed-out in the time allotted at a FHDRA Hearing, (especially if the mother has been slow coming forward with CDA) so an extra hearing may be necessary to get a full workable set of Directions.

The court bundle for a Fact-Finding Hearing is mostly the same as that for a Final Hearing, in terms of headings and index, (see later), but with the addition of a 'Scott Schedule'. This is a table that clearly sets out allegations and cross-allegations, with each numbered, and with responses each party makes to each. In addition, there are usually witness statements from each party, but these only concern the allegations and not the application for child arrangements. The contents and court rules concerning court bundles used in this and the Final Hearing are the same, and are detailed in **Practice Directions 27A. For details of these online see Appendix IV.**

7c. Fact-Finding Hearing (if necessary)

These are at least day-long affairs, and some can go on for weeks. At the conclusion, a Judge gives a narrative judgment which should be converted into writing by the Court Office. Importantly the Judge should give a decision on at least some of the numbered allegations in the Scott Schedule, about who was telling the truth or if they are undetermined. Do not be surprised if a Judge only decides on some of the items in a Scott Schedule and leaves others with no comment.

After dealing with the Fact-Finding a Judge may go straight on to make further Directions for the main application at the next hearing. For example, the Judge may consider the court needs a further report from CAFCASS, usually a report according to Children Act 1989 Part I section 7, (AKA a Section 7 report) based upon what facts have been decided did or did not happen.

It is at this hearing that the court may appoint a Guardian to represent a child or children, as parties to the proceedings, in light of any facts found – for example, if it is found that both parents have behaved negligently towards them. Any such Guardian is given Legal Aid for a solicitor and barrister who are supposed to represent the unbiased interests of the child or children, although in practice they can side totally with a resident parent (nearly always the mother). On the other hand, an existing Children's Guardian, appointed because of the severity of allegations by both parties, could at this point be dismissed. Further, a party can at this point use the facts found to remove Legal Aid from the other party, (or get it for themself) and, in theory, these same facts found can be used in a 'form FL403 application' to remove an injunction.

8. Second CAFCASS report [Time delay: usually Final Hearing minus one to two weeks]

I have never attended a CAP Family Court case where a Section 7 report was not done. If the case follows a negative Fact-Finding it will undoubtedly be done – but only after the Fact-Finding summary has been written and any Activity Directions are completed.

A CAFCASS Section 7 report is often the most important document in a CAP court case. Because of its importance to a court the headings typically used in such reports are worth considering (**see Appendix V**). If a social worker does interview you to write a

Section 7 report, (and again, as a father don't be surprised if they don't), it is worth bearing in mind the sections of the standard report, for example, as a way of framing your answers, or as a way of questioning their understanding of the situation under each heading. One of the key things to remember is that this report makes a conclusion (recommendation) on an application, before the court does. A court will usually follow this recommendation to some degree, if not totally, and has to have a very compelling reason to go against it.

Fact-Findings and Section 7 reports are known as the two main mechanisms for prejudice in Family Court CAP cases. As a father do not be surprised if information gathering for this report seems grossly unfair. It is worth raising objections to this unfairness, but only in writing, so this can be added to a court bundle. Verbally arguing with a social worker involved in this process, or at any time, is always a mistake.

9. DRA [Time delay: all depends on preceding steps]

The best situation for a DRA (Dispute Resolution Appointment) hearing is where all the paperwork has been submitted to the court. This should include both parties' written and exchanged witness statements and CAFCASS' final report, (so their view on statements and the applications is known). If there has been a Fact-Finding the outcome of that should also be known, and any expert reports should already be done. At this point, therefore, one party should know if they are on a losing wicket. That party should then agree an out-of-court agreement, to turn the DRA into an effective Final Hearing, with the agreement being the substance of a Final Order.

The other extreme is where CAFCASS has held off making their final recommendations, and neither party has submitted their witness statements, (or if they have they want to submit new ones), the Fact-Finding is not conclusive, and both parties are even more entrenched in their determination to win. Even if this is the situation, one party usually knows he or she is likely to lose. It is, therefore, common for the DRA to turn into an advocacy-battlefield where extra things are argued for by one party, such as more expert reports, in the hope that this will pull their case out of the fire.

If no Final Order is possible at this hearing, the case is then listed for a Final Hearing. An Interim Order will give full details of the documents to be produced for this last hearing and, if pressed, the court can include Directions that detail a timetable for the exchange of documents between parties. There are Court Practice Directions that define this timetable, but getting things spelt-out in an Interim Order can be important for a LiP when faced with a legal expert on the other side, or an unrepresented and uncooperative ex-wife or partner.

10. Final Hearing bundle [Time delay: Final Hearing date minus four days]

Before a Final Hearing, the Applicant has to prepare a paginated bundle of documents for all sides as well as the Judge. However, if an Applicant is a LiP this task falls to the party who has a solicitor, be it the Respondent or Guardian. In hotly contested hearings, or where only one side has a legal team, (and the other does not), it can be the subject of much gamesmanship.

A court bundle is all the papers in a court case set out in an organised way, according to some pretty strict rules which detail such things as what documents belong in each of several sections, font size, line spacing, the number of pages that can be used, and length of paragraphs for different documents. All this detail is in the Family Court Practice Directions previously given (27A) and discussed in more depth in Chapter 13. Whoever prepares the bundle has to serve it on all parties, and will need to produce **at least four copies**: one for the Judge, one for the witness box, one for the other party, and one for themselves. **NB:** Where both parties are LiPs then a bundle may be prepared, at least in part, by the Court Office.

11. Final Hearing [Time delay: Government Directives have stipulated any Family Court case should take no longer than three months from the initial application. More typical is nine months to two years]

Final Hearings are rarely less than a day long. This is a trial, or contested hearing, where both parties give evidence under oath in support of their witness statements and are able to challenge parts of the other person's statement(s) by asking them questions. This hearing is all about advocacy. It first involves each witness speaking to their lawyer (if they have one) about their written statement. Then each witness must answer questions from the Judge and the other party, or the other party's lawyer, after which their lawyer will 're-cross' with questions, if they think their client has said something unclear or contradictory. When a LiP is without a barrister, the initial questioning and re-cross is tricky to accomplish. Instead of answering questions from their lawyer (which usually takes up only a short time), they can make an open-ended statement. However, it is unclear how a LiP is supposed to re-cross, to clarify something they said in reply to the other party or their lawyer.

As replies are given the Judge takes notes of comments made, to use in his judgment, and so do the barristers, but for other reasons. For at the end of all this questioning the barristers have the final task of 'making submissions'. This is when they get up and try and weave an argument to say why their client's application should be given, based on what is written, and based on what people said as witnesses (and in this they need to quote key phrases). A LiP-advocate has to do this difficult job themselves, although a Judge can suggest that parties make their final submissions in writing (if the witnesses' testimonies finish at the end of a court day) in which event on the next day he reads these before making his or her judgment.

Finally, the Judge is given, by either side in the application, sometimes via a document in the court bundle and sometimes verbally, a 'reading list'. This is a list of bits of the court bundle each side wants the Judge to re-read in support of their position.

12. Order(s) [Time delay: Final Hearing date plus zero to five days]

At the end of a case a Judge often uses the barristers in a courtroom to help draft the wording of a Final Order. If you don't have a barrister you should nevertheless attempt to add in your comments at this point. Broadly speaking, get as much detail as possible about things that are in your favour, and as little as possible about negative things (and a trick here is just to be silent). Orders, even when written by professionals, are usually open to interpretation, and this can work against you (if not specific enough) or in your favour, if the wording is vague. **For more on what to do if you lose your court case go to chapter 14.**

If you win you almost certainly will want a clear Section 8 Child Arrangement Order, but there may be other orders that could help you. Conversely, you may find yourself asking for things over which a Judge cannot make an order. It is, therefore, worth knowing all the types of orders that can be made under the law in which you made your application. (**NB:** A Final Court Order is accompanied by a court stamp and is dated; don't confuse Final Orders with drafts, which can change). **See Appendix I – all the orders you can make under Private Family Law Child Arrangement Case within the Children Act 1989 Part I & II.**

Even if you lose an application, or counter application as the Respondent, you should not walk out of the court in a huff. Much can be gained in the use of the right words in a Court Order, so it pays to stick around in the courthouse until all of the other party's team have left – in case they try some last-minute amendments to an order by consulting a Judge in Chambers, or via a very short extra hearing.

6

Options for a Litigation Team

As a McKenzie Friend, one of the hardest things I find is getting a father to make a budget, (of time and money), for a court case. Agreed, there are a lot of unknowns and the figures involved can have a broad range, but this is the way of many projects. Often the reason for this reluctance is that a father feels his court case ought to be for free, or not happen at all, because what a mother is proposing is so clearly wrong. Also, child arrangement disputes nearly always hit men when they are most financially distressed. While a mother may view separation as a chance for a new start, maybe with a new partner, or in a home without someone she has come to hate or resent, for a father it is all chaos and destruction of a lifetime's work. A father is often renting a new home for himself while paying maintenance, the mortgage for his wife and children's home, as well as court costs for a divorce – if he is one of a diminishing number of men still willing to marry in the UK.

Another reason fathers duck-and-dive from budgeting is what I call the 'Family Court Stockholm Syndrome'. A father traumatised at the prospect of losing his right to bring up his children can find himself surrounded by people accepting this as normal. As a result, just like people who in a high stress situation side with criminals, known as the Stockholm Syndrome, a father can start to doubt his own judgment – at least enough to make him not want to commit any money.

The solution is often a simple conversation. For if a father really believes the child arrangements proposed by his ex will be bad for his kids, putting aside what it will do to him, what choice does he have but to go to court if the mother will not compromise? Furthermore, it is self-evidently an abuse to deny any child shared-parenting. This is both in terms of exposing a child to the risks of developmental harm, (that science now attributes to an absence of shared-parenting after family break-ups), and the inhumanity of alienating a child from a loving parent.

I have already outlined the sort of people who can help you run a successful court case, as well as what processes are involved in a Child Arrangement Order. It is now decision time. **Do not go any further without deciding a budget and a litigation team!**

To help I discuss here the options for a team, which aren't many, as well as the statistics of what others do. I tackle getting things for free, and its pitfalls, later on.

USING A FULL LEGAL TEAM

You will know if you have enough savings to afford a legal professional for all or some of your case, for you cannot possibly pay them out of your salary (a solicitor's hourly fees are about 20 times that of an average man's hourly wage). Solicitors' costs account for at least 80 per cent of the overall spend on a court case as in the UK, unlike elsewhere, there is no legislation preventing solicitors charging members of the public at business rates. Government figures give a range in London, from a junior to a senior lawyer, of £179–490 per hour and outside of London the cheapest areas still have lawyers raking in £130–235 per hour, (by extrapolating from the *Solicitor's Guideline Hourly Rates* [2010, HM Courts and Tribunal Service]).

Try as you might, solicitors are unlikely to predict how many hours will be needed and do not offer fixed-price deals. As a father, you consequently have to balance the need to ensure the judicial process does not rob your children of their right to be brought up by their natural father, and your need to avoid financial ruin, (so that even if you won you could not provide a home). It sounds simple on paper, but in real life it can be one of the most testing times a man ever has to face.

The benefits of using a solicitor include: that it frees you up to gather and search for evidence to support your case, it ensures you avoid legal red-herrings and using solicitors will give you a chance to just get on with your life. There is also some evidence that court cases take less time when both parties have representation (1) as compared to when both parties are LiPs. As in the latter situation, a lot of time can be wasted showing up to hearings without the right paperwork.

Even if you opt for a solicitor I suggest you continue to read this and other books on how to be a LiP. I also recommend asking to be copied on everything your solicitor sends and receives, as well as what you send them, and they send you, and periodically ask for copies of everything they have 'on file'. The reason for this advice is that, just like builders, lawyers can overrun budgets. Such overspending can lead to a parting of ways and you then have to pick-up the running. Getting papers out of a lawyer you have dropped is like getting blood out of a wilfully bloody-minded stone. If you already have all these papers, and have also been following the technicalities of your case, you will be far better equipped if you find yourself in court alone.

I am often asked how you get a good lawyer. If I had the answer to this I would be a millionaire. One thing that might help you decide is whether a firm specialises in Family Law alone, or does a bit of everything. There are some other pointers such as if they are a member of Resolution, or if they are on the Children Panel Board. Personal recommendations are also suggested by many. However, solicitors who are good with one case can be useless at the next. What is more, they lie. Most of what is written on professional websites, like the Law Society's site for solicitors, are just wish lists of work they want. You could find yourself lumbered with a firm who, despite what they said at the beginning, get most of their work from fighting fathers or doing Public Family Law work for social services. Such firms, as soon as an objection is raised by the other side, often just give in and tut-tut at you for being a bad father.

As a rule of thumb, there is little correlation between what you pay and what you get back from a solicitor. Of course, lawyers will argue strenuously to the contrary. Yet, the professional bodies for lawyers keep no league tables of performance. There is no calibration done to compare one law firm, or one barrister, against another. This would anyway, I'm sure lawyers would argue, be pointless as, apart from the overcharging element you have in all professional work, legal work is a bit like marketing. If you have the wrong product spending a pile on advertising still isn't going to sell much. In the same way, a top lawyer cannot undo the facts of, or the adverse situation in, a court case.

My advice is, therefore, to get things as cheaply as you can, but not to ground the whole venture over a few pennies. There are limits, which brings me on to the use of Family Law Legal Executives (LEs), or one-man solicitors, with rights of audience. I tried using a one-stop-shop LE firm, who were going to be far cheaper than a solicitor and barrister, or a direct access barrister. I remember having to hop up three flights of stairs to an office above a Kebab house as I was on crutches with a broken leg. I waited for three hours for a pre-booked meeting with the LE, but in the end went away not having seen him. The problem is that while firms of solicitors are resourced to backup hundreds of cases per solicitor, a one-man-band that does court work and administration is going to be a real mess, even though they are cheap.

Solicitors need money on account, although they can extend credit as work progresses. I would allow a bare minimum of £20,000 for a typical straightforward case, and at least £2-3,000 of this needs to be reserved for the final hearing, (including the barrister's fee) assuming this lasts just one day. It would be foolish to spend your budget on getting to the trial and then having to represent yourself on the final day – and without planning this does happen.

A LITIGATION TEAM WITHOUT A SOLICITOR

The only real alternative to using a solicitor is to instruct a direct access barrister and do the litigation work of a solicitor yourself, or with the help of a McKenzie Friend (who could also help you handle some hearings as a LiP-advocate). This sort of team has the potential of massive savings over a full legal team as it cuts out the need to pay two lawyers, and cuts out the most expensive one of the pair. Under this arrangement a LiP carries out the work of sending and receiving correspondence, dealing with the court, and the other party or their solicitor. A good McKenzie Friend, or a good self-help book, can then be used to guide the management of paperwork, and to help in deciding tactics and other applications needed in between hearings.

However, it is a mistake to think this is an easy option. Once you forgo a solicitor, litigation becomes a very lonely, stressful and time-consuming endeavour. While you may have a barrister in mind, or you have already prepped one in a conference for initial advice, the relationship is not the same as with a solicitor. Barristers are not accessible at all until an agreed paid-for-in-advance meeting. They will try and accommodate you once they have started with you, but their contracts of engagement make it clear they cannot guarantee to be at a hearing if other work takes them away, for example, if another court case overruns. Barristers work day-by-day and are not yours in the sense of a solicitor as they have no administrative backup – and it is a mistake to think that the clerks to the Chambers fulfil this function.

If the other party has a solicitor, and they find out that you are a LiP, you are going to be mistreated. Without the benefit of a solicitor's advice, you can waste money and effort on pointless activities, and the other party's solicitor will know this and even game you over irrelevancies. Solicitors also use tactics with a LiP that they would never employ with another solicitor, such as lying about things that were sent and delaying giving you copies until the very last minute (even up to the moment you walk into court). Preparing bundles with the other side legally represented is particularly fraught with tricks.

Dealing with a Family Law Court Office as a LiP can also be a headache. When you ask about the correct form, or process, or timescales, or even costs, they can cut you off with a parting comment that they: "Cannot give legal advice" – even when legal advice is not what you were asking.

To economise LiPs often use direct access barristers at only some hearings, fielding the rest themselves. Interim hearings can be very short — 20 or 30 minutes in front of a Judge — and if you have a barrister, you would still have to pay a full-day rate. **However, the**

problem then becomes in which hearings do you use a barrister and in which do you speak for yourself (and remember a McKenzie Friend cannot do the talking)?

It is a massive mistake to think you only need to pour resources into the Final Hearing, or that you can sway a Judge with a good Final Hearing testimony in the witness box. Such verbal evidence by both parties (Applicant or Respondent) tends to be low down on the list of deciding factors. More importantly, Judges, and parties to a case, work towards building an inescapable conclusion in the pieces of written evidences contained in the Final Hearing bundle, as argued for in a series of preliminary hearings. You should note that only things the court agrees with can be included in this bundle, so you can't slip in what you want. Also, only things in a court bundle can be talked about in the Final Hearing. You cannot hijack the court with new evidence presented at the last moment, or even talk about something that is not already in your written statement(s). Therefore, not having good advocacy in the interim hearings can damage a case in a way that a barrister, only brought in at the end, cannot possibly undo.

Conversely, fathers desperate to overturn child arrangements devised by a mother who has stolen resident-parent status, (sometimes by use of injunctions), can blow a disproportionate amount of their funds on an expensive barrister at the start of a case, in the hope of getting an interim order – such as an order to see their kids at all! However, if domestic abuse is raised in the proceedings, by either party, Practice Direction 12J comes into play. In this Para 6 stipulates that no interim order can effect a change in child arrangements, even by consent of both parents, until a social worker makes an initial safety report on the children named in the application (and both parties need to attend this hearing before an interim order changing child arrangements is made).

Yet, frequently fathers do not know if a CAFCASS/CAFCASS Cymru (Welsh equivalent) safety report has been completed. For this is typically researched by social workers speaking to the mother with whom the children reside (and claiming they phoned the father but he did not pick up). Also, fathers often do not even know if their ex has decided to use allegations of domestic abuse, (as the C1A may not have been given across or completed). As a result, using a good barrister at the FHDRA can be a disappointment and a waste of money, if the aim is for a father to see his kids by way of an interim order.

As a guide, if your case involves any of the situations listed under the section in this book *Should I ask a lawyer for initial advice?*, I would use a barrister at all your hearings (if you can afford them). If you, unfortunately, have a Fact-Finding Hearing scheduled ahead of a Final Hearing I would sacrifice all available funds, even those set aside for the Final Hearing, to fund a barrister at that hearing. Sell a kidney if you have to, but do not attend a Fact-Finding Hearing without employing a barrister.

A direct access barrister can charge anywhere from £500 to £5,000 (for a London QC) per day, and I am afraid you get the same thing whatever you pay. Barristers in out-of-London Chambers tend to be cheaper, and the cheapest I have ever had was £250 for a half-day. Barristers travel quite widely but you shouldn't have to pay their expenses for doing so. All of their charges are quoted ex-VAT, so add 20 per cent to get the real amount you will have to stomp up. This has to be paid in advance, along with signing a contract, per instruction.

The beauty of a legal team without a solicitor is you can potentially stretch your budget to cover extra things to boost your case, as and when needs develop. For example, if the court case takes a negative turn which necessitates you unexpectedly having to fund a report from an expert. These can be astonishingly expensive, especially if you need the expert who wrote the report to attend court.

Finally, I hope it is now clear that a McKenzie Friend can be one part of a litigation team, rather than a replacement for a legal team. McKenzie Friends used to charge rates set by the organisation FNF (Families Need Fathers), but nowadays they typically charge £15–60 per hour for each hour they do something, i.e. not for talking on the phone. Their fees are by way of compensation for lost earnings (and some can afford to do it for free). Amongst other things a McKenzie Friend can: help you prepare your documents for a court hearing, help take notes and remind you of points while you represent yourself in a hearing, negotiate with the other party in the court building, help you draft orders if an agreement or order is needed in the courtroom, help you with briefing a barrister, and assist in discussions with a Cafcass Officer.

WHAT TO DO WHEN YOU DISAGREE WITH YOUR LEGAL TEAM

Using legal experts is always an ordeal. Apart from anything else they drain your life savings and charge many times the rate most of us are paid. Court cases over who gets to bring up a father's children, or whether a father is ever going to see his children again, can bring a man to the edge of insanity. A father's need to win can therefore be at sharp odds with the blasé approach of those who do this sort of thing all the time. In addition, it can be difficult to speak to a solicitor, who often hides behind a wall of paralegals.

However, you have to remember that however much you are paying someone it does not mean you own them. Like any professional, solicitors hire themselves out by the hour, to try and achieve an agreed result, **but** done in a way they think is best for getting to that end-goal. What is more, solicitors, just like builders, multiplex jobs together, so you cannot always get to speak with them just when you want.

Although you may try and exercise constraint, things can boil over. There then arises the question of what to do if you fall out with a lawyer during a case. I can tell you what not to do: never try switching solicitor firms in the middle of a live court case (where hearings have been scheduled). Also, complaining to a professional body as a way of resolving things is a complete waste of time and effort. These organisations, The Law Society for solicitors and the Bar Council for barristers, are primarily there for the benefit of their members. They set criteria for entry to their professions, organise CPD, set ways of working with other parts of the judiciary and other such things. What they are not is a free alternative to litigation against your lawyer. Sometimes these organisations offer a dispute mediation service, but they are more concerned with patterns of behaviour of law firms across many clients, unless your complaint is about gross misconduct e.g. sex in return for work, or disclosure of confidential information. In terms of helping you during a court case, the complaint processes of professional bodies simply do not work fast enough.

However, if a law firm wants to leave you, but you disagree, the lawyer must get the permission of the court to withdraw – once you are past the first hearing of a case. What is more, not paying lawyers' bills, although it may ensure poor quality work, is not reason enough in the eyes of a court for a legal expert to abandon their client. Lawyers are up to their eyeballs in insurances anyway, so this is unlikely to hurt them.

One of the most common complaints I hear about legal experts is that they do not listen to what you want, or do what you ask. It is true that some solicitors and barristers just mechanically go through things in a standard way. However, sometimes a lawyer knows what the client is asking simply won't work in court or what is being asked is contrary to their role as officers of the court. You have to remember that a court case is not about the real-world facts of your life, but about a paraphrasing of it, a cartoon outline. What you think is a killer-counter-argument for an accusation in the real world may be of no use given legal rules and laws. Further, Family Law is never about the welfare of the father. So if you feel your lawyers are not looking after what you want and need, this can be because that is what the law dictates.

If you leave your lawyers because you have run out of money or because they have gone over budget, that is fair enough. Yet, leaving a solicitor in the middle of litigation over a difference of opinion is a significant move, and more often than not a major mistake. Always look for a second view, from a barrister or a McKenzie Friend (not another solicitor), before ditching a solicitor in this way. As an example, in one case I was involved with the respondent-mother produced a document she claimed showed the father had lost his PR over their child in a foreign court. The father knew that this was a fraud, and produced the real document, translated into English. The solicitors insisted on not disputing this point, which led to the father having countless stand-up rows with them. In the end, the Judge in the case did not care about PR in another country, whether it was in place or not.

The situation with removing barristers is more straightforward as you only contract them on a daily basis. Never, ever, dismiss a barrister at court. Trust me on this one. If you think a barrister is not doing a good job with your case do not use them at the next hearing or, if in the middle of testimony, you will have a chance to put your story when you are in the witness box. It is then that you can contest anything that your barrister said, or anyone else said.

I hope it is clear that while you do not own those you employ as legal experts you are wedded to what they do. Being stuck with someone else's case-strategy is the main driver for not using a firm of solicitors. Family Courts are full of prejudice against fathers and the more bitter a family dispute the more this prejudice shows itself. Many legal firms practising Family Law have no answers for this bias and make most of their money either defending mothers or working for social services. Putting yourself in a position of being able to swap experts in-and-out after each stage of your Family Court proceedings at least gives you the chance to try new ways of addressing the obstacles you encounter in your particular court case.

A LITIGANT ON HIS LONESOME

Paying for a solicitor can be an extravagance, as the processes of the Family Courts are uncomplicated by legal standards. However, unless your case is about something straightforward, or you know for sure a court is predisposed towards you, for example, because of a report you have from CAFCASS, or because the mother has abandoned the family, a father running a Family Court case without **any** help is just foolish.

It is entirely feasible for a well-educated man, with a comprehensive computer system, to handle court paperwork for a full contested hearing on his own, even if this means producing the court bundles (see chapter 13). However, where the proposition of not spending any money at all fails is in advocacy. Speaking in court is a skill that takes a particular type of person, and a good deal of training, to accomplish.

Is this book going to leave me hanging on how to represent myself in court?

If you mean how to successfully speak, question witnesses, and make final submissions to a Judge without anyone to help you, then yes. It's just like trying to learn to drive using a correspondence course; there is nothing I can write that can prepare you for such a task. The whole idea of a McKenzie Friend was born out of this problem: how do you do your own advocacy? Of course, in many hearings nowadays both parties are unrepresented, so in these it may seem you have a chance of saving money. Yet, as I repeatedly say in this book, Family Courts work against fathers and help mothers. A father needs to employ a stronger litigation team than a mother – unless, as said before, you know the court has already sided with you.

I cannot tell you how many times I have heard of fathers who are strident on the merits of their case, and dismissive of the other party's evidence and story, easily give ground as a LiP-advocate. In the moment they seem to perceive themselves as demonstrating reasonableness, (or more likely their mind just turns to mush when hit with public speaking). Giving in, or failing to argue any point coherently, merely highlights to a court that you are an advocacy-pushover, and your case is therefore sunk.

It's not all about your ability either. Quite apart from the general prejudice in the Family Court system, there is additional reasoning that undermines a father speaking in front of a Judge. For if a father asks for an order to have his children live with him, then he must be irresponsible if he cannot even afford legal representation. Or, if he can demonstrate he does have money to bring up his children, then his case must have no merits as otherwise someone would be representing him. A woman in the same situation is seen differently. For a mother asking to bring up her children on her own, but not having enough money for legal representation, is understandable, as she may typically rely on the children's father for an income.

Any LiP who does his own advocacy in court is also viewed as having strong personal interests in the issues before a Judge and therefore not in any way objective, or of any use to the Judge. Further, if a father is confronting the additional obstacle of CDA, the case he has to fight will be very different from that of a mother, who has victimhood as a birthright.

There are a whole bunch of rules for barristers concerning how they can phrase questions to a witness, and as a LiP-advocate you have to try and follow these same strictures. In basics, there has to be a question in what you say and not just an accusation, and you have to refer a witness to the exact page and paragraph in the court bundle when asking them something about what was said or written by them or someone else. If the answer given in reply avoids the point you wanted to make, then you have to ask the question again, putting it more directly. I suggest reading the book: *How to Represent Yourself in the Family Court*, by Jason M. Hadden and Rhiannon Davies, [2015, Little Brown Book Group]. This volume is a crushingly naïve self-help guide, written from the viewpoint of a barrister and solicitor. However, it is also guides you through court processes including how to question and speak in court. **NB:** Litigants in Person in Scottish courts fare much better, with their equivalent of a McKenzie Friend, a Lay Helper, being able to speak in court. However, it is strictly forbidden for such help to receive payment for their service, unlike in the UK.

Most fathers who do not have, or cannot afford, a solicitor may find themselves having to speak for themselves at some point in their court case. A McKenzie Friend at your side is meant to help, by using a series of hushed discussions about points in a case. Such assistance can work to a degree, but it is slow and usually cannot keep up with the demands of a Judge. Yet, without anyone at your side, advocacy is a big-ask. For an amateur, it is something in which you are more likely to fail than succeed.

The conclusion of a 2014 study conducted for the Ministry of Justice (9) is that very few LiPs at all can cope with every aspect of a Family Court case on their own, with any sort of success. For at the end of the day, running a case is like a card game. You can read up on how to play, and study the best ways to win as much as you like, but there is no substitute for actually playing hands. Some get lucky, but that is all.

The advice for a LiP forced into going it alone, because they have no money at all and do not qualify for Legal Aid (see chapter ten), is within the theme of this whole book i.e. **prepare as much as possible before you start a case.** Don't just dash-off a C100 form in the hope it will change things, somehow. Also, have a backstop position, and look for all and any opportunities to use this in courthouse situations (see chapter two). Phone conversations with a McKenzie Friend, especially those who can work for free, can help with both of these strategies.

WHAT OTHER PEOPLE DO

The UK Family Courts hear over a quarter-of-a-million cases per year, which since 2014 are now held in dedicated Family Courts within special centres, (although other types of courts may use the courtroom itself). According to the Ministry of Justice figures (1) the percentage of applicants who were legally represented dropped from 77 per cent, in 2012, to 52 per cent, in 2017. 'Legally represented' in these statistics means having someone 'on the court record', i.e. a solicitor doing the litigation. The figure of 52 per cent was made up of cases in which only the Applicant was represented: 32 per cent; and those cases where both the Applicant and the Respondent were legally represented: 20 per cent. The year 2017 was in fact a record high for Private Law Family Cases under the Children Act in which neither party was legally represented, at 37 per cent of all cases.

However, these statistics do not take into account the different grades of 'not being legally represented'. For example, there is no record of how many litigants who didn't use a solicitor instead used a direct access barrister, or a McKenzie Friend.

There are also no numbers on the effect of legal representation, full or partial, on the outcome of a court case. It is known that there is no relationship between the education or employment of a LiP and their success in handling their case without a solicitor – in other words, being well-educated or higher-paid doesn't mean you fare better in the Family Courts. Further, despite how Judges see things, the merits of a court case do not correlate with whether a party is legally represented or not. In other words, contrary to a commonly held axiom, fathers do not typically turn up to court unrepresented because their case has been turned down by lawyers.

A study into the motivations and conditions of LiPs, commissioned by the Ministry of Justice, (9) across 165 Family Law court cases, found that twice as many LiPs without any legal team were the respondent, and a woman. Litigant-fathers with no help at all, were far rarer. Of those fathers that did not have legal representation, three-quarters lacked the money to pay for it or had failed to secure Legal Aid (a group with a typical profile of a man in his twenties, on benefits, or a low wage). Therefore, only a quarter of the litigant-fathers without legal representation had no legal help out of choice. However, even within this quarter, half had some legal help even if it did not last the whole court case. This means that out of all fathers in the Family Courts, only six per cent had no legal help by choice.

I would sub-divide this unrepresented 'by choice' group of fathers, out of my own experience. I would say it firstly consists of those fathers driven mad or desperate at losing their children. Having made one application and failed to get an order they needed, such fathers make a series of further applications to try and correct and amend the first one. In their hearts, they know these applications have little chance and so they refuse to waste any more money on them. They tend also to ask McKenzie Friends to make an appeal, or get an interim order of contact. Such people can also be very active in Father Support Groups.

The second type of 'by choice' litigant-fathers without legal help, perhaps one to two per cent of all cases, are what I call 'chancers'. These have no interest in the detail of a court process, and no interest in spending money on it, but simply want to have as many opportunities as possible to get in front of a Judge and argue for their children in whatever way comes into their head. They usually employ a shotgun technique of making many applications to the courts, as well as many approaches to McKenzie Friends on any list they can find – usually giving only a day or so notice. I often find myself questioning the sincerity of this last small grouping, (who seem to confirm the negative preconceptions Judges of father-litigants-in-person).

IN CONCLUSION

With a rise of women with no legal representation, and a rise of men with little representation, in combination with other 2014 changes, such as the new CAP rules that emphasise dispute resolution, the nature of the Family Courts has changed. Many people are now experiencing a process that is simply both parties settling matters at the first hearing with the help of a Cafcass worker, or a Judge, who shapes an agreement which then becomes an order. What effect kicking out lawyers in so many court cases will have on justice for fathers, longer-term, is debatable. At one level if a father was only going to get what a mother wanted from a court case, however much it was prolonged, then it is better to get this done and dusted quickly and without spending a lot.

In my opinion, if a litigant-father needs to effect a change in the way his children are brought up following his separation from their mother, who is resisting these changes, he needs to be tooled-up with the right legal team before resorting to the Family Courts. I personally believe that a father faced with the uphill battle of tackling prejudice in the court system is not well-served by the extraordinary female dominance found in firms of Family Law solicitors. That is not to say that all such solicitors hate or undermine fathers, or that they are all feminist extremists – far from it. However, with such single-gender prevalence in the training and practice of this profession there exists an almost total myopia of the issues faced by fathers, let alone any will or ability to be creative in the defence of fathers' applications to parent their children – and this applies to the work of both male and female solicitors of Family Law. I believe it is often best for a father to devise his own legal argument for his court case, and then hand this to legal experts to implement. Further, this legal team should always include a barrister for use in at least some of his hearings.

My advice about finding a good barrister is the same about finding a good solicitor: if only there was such a source! There is an online directory of direct access barristers on the Bar Council's website (the overseeing professional body for barristers). Confusingly, these are listed by name and not Chambers. I would ask around Father Support Groups for news of where to get the best deals, and if not, just search on Google Maps and then ring up the nearest Barrister's Chambers and ask the Chief Clerk to the Chambers if they have anyone who does direct access Family Law, but be prepared to give specific dates for meetings and court appearances.

However, the drain on a person's life also needs to be taken into account. If you can afford it, and if your case is complex, involves claims of severe domestic abuse, has a substantial international element, involves Public Law, or is in the High Courts, then a legal team with a solicitor is maybe what you need.

Works cited, but not referenced in the text

9.   **Trinder, Liz; Hunter, Rosemary; Hitchings, Emma; Miles, Joanna; Moorhead, Richard; Smith, Leanne; Sefton, Mark; Hinchly, Victoria; Bader, Kay; Pearce, Julia:** *Litigants in person in private family law cases.* [S.l. Ministry of Justice, (2014)].

1.   *Family Court Statistics Quarterly, England and Wales, Annual 2017 October to December.* [S.l. Ministry of Justice, (29th March, 2018)].

7

Setting the Context I –
Misandrist Family Laws & Interpretations

"All animals are equal, but some animals are more equal than others." *Animal Farm* by George Orwell [Secker and Warburg, London, England, 1945].

Before embarking on litigation, I suggest reflecting on the context of Private Family Law court action. This should include a more in-depth understanding of the written word of law, and how the Family Courts institutionalise it. For despite the negative way these courts treat fathers compared to mothers in all family matters, whether about children or property, it is often hard for those who have experienced this to convey, to those who have not, how it is so discriminatory and yet still legal.

Discrimination in the courts is officially denied by all those making a good living out of family disputes, which leaves a bunch of amateurs to try and explains things. Yet, charities that have arisen in the UK to fight the stripping of children from fathers have all grappled to put their collective finger on the key instrument of discrimination, which in the end is often delivered by another man sitting as a Judge. For there is a myriad of inequalities in the words used in law, presumptions of law, Court Practice Directives and informal (unwritten) decisions of Judicial Study Boards that together build a consistent prejudice. A prejudice implemented through a quite sickening relay between social services and Judges, who pass the baton of wrong-doing between them.

I suggest in the next three chapters only a few of the inequalities found in Family Law and court practices which can be used to prevent men from being fathers – simply because a mother wants it that way. However, there are many more inequalities and consequences than I have room to mention here.

THE FORMAL STUFF

There are several types of rules that restrict or affect the decisions a court can make. 'Statutes' are Acts of Law passed by that branch of Government known as Parliament, i.e. the elected House of Commons and the unelected House of Lords. The most relevant Statutory Law for fathers trying to get shared residency of their children is the Children Act 1989 (CA 1989). Although this is changed from its initial state by a series of amendments, most recently the Children and Families Act 2014, it is still called the Children Act 1989. This Act, in current and previous versions, is available to **view online at the Legislation.gov.uk website, (details are given in Appendix IV).** Be warned there are tabs on this site for 'current' and 'previous versions' of Law Acts, so make sure you are looking at the current one. You also need to be mindful that the website is not updated automatically, and can be out of date. Finally, a Law Act may be present but may not yet have come into force (and usually this is done by the first order under an Act or by passing a specific date). Also relevant is the Statute that tells Judges what they can and cannot do in general: the Senior Courts Act 1981. When a court's decision contradicts a relevant Statute, it is potentially an error in law although this has to be decided by a Court of Appeal.

In addition to Statutes, there is Case Law, also called Common Law. The idea behind these two types of Statutes is that law is formed from both Law Acts and the interpretation of these laws by senior Judges sitting in the High Courts. Finally, these same High Courts can decide on things not covered by Law Acts under something called Inherent Jurisdiction. These precedents made in judgments within High Court and Appeal Court cases are in theory binding on lower Judges. Case Law can be searched online via the website for the British and Irish Legal Information Institute, or Bailii for short, **(details of this site are in Appendix IV).** There are a plethora of amateur sites that also offer this information, but Bailii is the main trusted source.

At this point, a lot of fathers and campaigners can get very excited as High Court cases and Appeal Court cases are publicly available, even though they are under Family Law (which imposes confidentiality on case details). Summaries of such cases are seen by many fathers'-rights campaigners and lobbyists as a window into the minds of the senior judiciary, and often appear to give new helpful points of law for fathers in their court cases. These summaries can also seem to prove the prejudicial nature of the whole Family Court institution.

However, this excitement about Case Law can be misplaced. Firstly, for a case-history decision to be relevant to a new case the two have to be identical in their detail. However, not all of this detail is in published summaries and in any event, whether two cases are equivalent in law is a matter of opinion. Secondly, for every case decision that decides the rule of law in one way, there can be other cases that give a different decision. Thirdly, there is a difference between general remarks by a Judge, what are called 'Obiter Remarks', and decisions on principles of law. Obiter Remarks have no relevance either to any other court case or to prejudices across the whole of Family Law. What matters is the key principle of law decided, what is known as the 'Ratio Decidendi', sometimes just called 'The Ratio'.

Unpicking The Ratio from Obiter Remarks, and the relevance of a Higher Court Case to another hearing, is something that is best left to a solicitor or barrister. As a LiP, I would not advise using Case Law more than once in a hearing. When I have seen this done there is usually a painful silence and shuffling of feet, as what it often shows is that there is a big difference in calibre from High Court Judges to Lower Court Judges. Often Case Law is simply dismissed without explanation if presented by a LiP. Where a legal expert publishes Case Law as proving a particular legal point, then you can use it – however, even then, you have to understand why the Case Law says what authorities say it says and be prepared to defend that proposition.

As well as the above two types of the law, courts are also governed by Procedural Rules or Practice Directions (PDs). These too are approved by the elected Parliament of the country in some form or other. Collectively these are called Secondary Legislation, which is brought into existence and amended by documents called 'Statutory Instruments'. The relevant rules of the Family Court are the Family Procedure Rules 2010 and the supporting Practice Directions. Within these PDs, the most important may be the Family PD 12B – Child Arrangements Programme. This PD is a set of rules on the court process to follow when settling disputes about who looks after children and when. You will often see barristers thumbing through a little black book which contains these PDs in condensed form. When a court case does not follow relevant procedural rules it is potentially an unlawful hearing, although this would need to be decided by a Court of Appeal.

Finally, there are the influences on the courts, which are often quoted in summations of High Court cases. One such influence are the books of guidance. For behind each set of Law Acts, the Civil Service creates manuals for those dealing with the legislation to follow. In the case of the CA 1989, there is a series from HMSO called *Children Act 1989 Guidance and Regulations*. There may be many more such publications for Judges and barristers as well, but generally these are hard to find as they are meant primarily for internal consumption.

HOW THE CA 1989 CHANGED FATHERHOOD

The first iteration of the CA 1989, in Section 2 (1), confirmed the prior status quo in Great Britain for people married, but through a new instrument called 'Parental Responsibility' (PR). This section of the Act automatically gives both married parents full, legal guardianship over their child, or children. Yet, this is the only significant part of the new Law Act that is gender neutral.

The situation for unmarried mothers in the UK is given in CA 1989 Section 2 (2) (a) which says a mother always gets PR over her child, regardless of whether she is married or not. However, unmarried fathers need to 'acquire' PR, by doing something relevant in law. For example, a father may marry the mother of his child after the birth of that child, in which case he automatically acquires PR (under the Legitimacy Act of 1976), even if the father's name is not shown on the child's birth certificate, (before or after marrying).

This point of law is something many people miss as the reference to the Legitimacy Act is well buried (i.e. CA 1989 4 (1A)a, refers to Births and Deaths Registration Act 1953 which in section 3 refers to the Family Law Reform Act 1987, which then refers in section 1(3)a to the Legitimacy Act). So contrary to what many authorities believe, and what fathers are frequently advised, if a father marries the mother of his children, before or after his child's birth, he acquires PR whether his name is on the birth certificate, or whether there is a PR Agreement or not. However, even though PR is given through a post-birth marriage, it is still not a right but something acquired with the permission of the mother (by her agreeing to marry the father).

Unmarried fathers who stay in a cohabiting-relationship are treated more harshly within the Children Act 1989, as they needed to get something more explicit. Such a father needs an agreement in the form of a Parental Responsibility Agreement with the mother of their children, or child, to register their name on their child's birth certificate, or re-register the child's birth certificate with their name included. In this situation, the mother has to be present at the Registrar Office, in the case of registering or re-registering a birth certificate, or at the Magistrates Court, in the case of a PR Agreement. The presence of the mother is needed, simply because under the CA 1989 an unmarried mother is a higher status parent than an unmarried father.

Along with others, fathers can also get PR for children by a Court Order. There are three types of such orders. If a father, or anyone else, applies and achieves a child arrangement order that says the child is to live with them for some or all of the time, then PR is automatically acquired (and here again a PR Agreement or name on a birth certificate does not matter). A court can also simply order PR be given to a father, usually as part of a more comprehensive child arrangement hearing. Finally, PR is automatic if a person adopts a child through a Family Court.

Apart from the perhaps subtle, but important, fact that fathers have no automatic, independent (of the other parent), legal rights over their biological children, there are other essential differences in the CA 1989. A father who acquires PR, however it is done, can have it removed in a Private Law application by the mother, or by his child. Whereas conversely, a mother's PR cannot be removed except by Public Law. What is more, if a biological father does not have PR, a mother can agree to an alternative father having PR without telling the biological father and without the need to go to court – by simply entering into a PR Agreement. Further, a father who marries the mother of his child after his child's birth cannot, without the mother's agreement, change the name on that child's birth certificate.

It has not always been this way. In the past, before the CA 1989, fathers could claim legal guardianship of their biological child under a rule of law whereby a man is accepted as the natural guardian of his child. The Legitimacy Act of 1976, Section 2, gave a route by which such fathers could then obliterate the past, by marrying a mother after a child's birth, (later modified to include civil partnerships), effectively giving a 'try before you buy' option. For once a child is legitimised, as long as someone, either a parent or the child, approached a Registrar Office within three months of such a marriage, the child's birth certificate could then be re-registered with the father's surname and his details in a new ledger entry.

I am one such child of this law. I have seen the ledger entry of my registration of birth in London's Central Records (at a time when you could visit and search records, unlike today). In those records only my father's surname is recorded, the previous entry having been expunged and hidden under Tippex. I have always had to cope with not having a birth certificate since the original was destroyed in all records; I can only have a copy of a record.

No special permission was needed for my father to become my legal guardian, not from a court or my mother, as providing and caring for a family of seven children was enough. When I was twelve, my father married my mother and legitimised all his children by her, and so removed all records of social stigma on how we came into being. My father's guardianship could not be removed by the wishes of either my mother, or me, but only by Court Order if my father had done something that came under the category of child neglect, which he did not do, (as few fathers do, then or now).

The Children Act 1989 took away the automatic rights of fathers to be fathers, as seen in section 2.4 (4):

"The rule of law that a father is the natural guardian of his legitimate child is abolished."

This change introduced an extra, **hidden**, step for fathers for a period of 1989 to 2002. During this time, unmarried fathers needed to have a PR Agreement, regardless of whether they were named on a child's birth certificate or not. Any child born after the date of 2002 is treated differently, as the law was changed so that naming a father on a birth certificate is now deemed as also agreeing to PR.

Yet, the only route for a father from 1989 to 2002 who had children outside of marriage was through either a Court Order or by the mother, (wife, girlfriend or partner, it didn't matter as they were treated the same), granting the father his rights. However, what usually happened was that neither parent of a cohabiting relationship knew of this new loophole until its effect came to bear on a situation. The typical situation was when their relationship had broken down and they were in a custody or child arrangements dispute. Before a breakdown in his relationship with his partner a typical cohabiting father, throughout the time he worked and provided for his family, usually thought himself the legal guardian of his children, whose birth certificates bore his name, in something he assumed was a 'common law marriage'.

I was tripped up by this loophole in 2007. I had returned to the UK with my son, who had been born abroad. I had already made him a naturalised British Citizen under a procedure run by the British Embassy abroad. My son had a British passport, Certificate of British Citizenship, and I was named on both his Foreign and British Birth Certificates as his father. His mother was a foreign national, on a visiting visa, whom I had not married, and so my son's claim to treatment as a British Citizen came from me alone.

My son arrived in a terrible sick condition and was on arrival immediately rushed into hospital. After a day or so, I was stopped from seeing him by a hospital administrator that demanded I pay £600 a day, backdated, for the intensive care unit as my son was not entitled to NHS care because I was not his legal guardian. I produced his British Citizenship certificate, his passport and his birth certificates that showed me as his father. She dismissed all of this and said that if I did not have PR, none of that counted. Of course, I had no idea at all what PR was and asked for an explanation, but instead was just forced to pay or have my son thrown into the streets. Later, I managed to get hold of a male senior administrator, and he explained the above distinction and quoted the law and directives to NHS administrators that were relevant, (which I now forget), and also helped me find out how to get PR. It was a crude and simple one sheet of paper that my partner and I signed in a jiffy and had stamped at the Magistrates Court, (and then I got my money back).

None of this would have happened if my partner and I had swapped genders.

CONTACT VS RESIDENT PARENT STATUS

Historically, the main use of the PR mechanism, (some would say its main design), is as a means to demote separated fathers to an inferior category of parenthood in any child custody and arrangements dispute. This distinction is necessary, in the eyes of Judges, because Family Courts did not, and still do not, recognise shared-residence of children as feasible following the separation of their parents.

In part, this prejudice against shared-residency is based on a personal feeling, by those who have not experienced it, that two homes will be unsettling for a child. In another part this prejudice comes from a dictate from the Civil Service in the manual *Children Act 1989 Guidance and Regulations, Volume 1, Court Orders*, published by HM Stationery Office in 1991, paragraph 2.2 (8) at page 10:

"[Regarding shared residency orders]… **it is not expected that it would become a common form of order, partly because most children will still need the stability of a single home, and partly because in the cases where shared care is appropriate there is less likely to be a need for the court to make any order at all.**"

In other words: 'shared-residence doesn't work, because we say so; and anyway if you're in court you've already disqualified yourself from getting shared-residence as you must be in a high-conflict dispute and therefore it will never work'.

I should warn that there is a lot of double-talk about the terms 'shared-residence' and 'shared-parenting'. Some take it to be what it says: a child having two homes. Others are more pedantic and take it to mean a child living with both parents for exactly equal amounts of time. Using the latter definition allows someone to argue that even when a child lives with a non-prime parent a lot of the time, it is still not shared-residence. So that person is still a 'contact parent' – with all the accompanying public and legal preconceptions.

Historically the law denies shared-residency for children in the original words used in the CA 1989, where it defines a Section 8 Order:

"**A contact order means an order requiring the person with whom a child lives, or is to live, to allow the child to visit or stay with the person named in the order, or for that person and the child otherwise to have contact with each other;**

A residence order means an order settling the arrangements to be made as to the person with whom a child is to live;"

The above section of the law divides parents as either a 'resident parent', or a 'contact parent', and it is not possible to have two in one category. Using this definition, Family Court Judges can infer that as fathers have inferior status under their PR entitlement, so they must be the contact parent **in all cases**. This is despite the closeness of relationships of a father with his son or daughter, despite who is the main breadwinner (in fact this matters least of all). Once a father is thus made a contact parent, he has already lost the right to bring up his children the way he wants before even getting into court.

Now I know the Children Act 1989 was amended by the Children and Families Act 2014, which removed the words 'resident' and 'contact' parent from the types of order, but it does not matter. As with all laws, it is the interpretation of the law by the courts that matters and the presumption of parents in dispute being either contact or resident parents **is still** what the law is interpreted as saying when making Section 8 Orders. All that happened in 2014, was a change of language. Nowadays, people call the contact-parent the non-resident-parent, and the resident-parent as the parent whom the child lives with most of the time. Contact-parent as a label, and using the words 'having contact' with children, persist and are certainly not outlawed in courts, or Court Orders.

Even if married to the mother at the time of their children's birth, fathers are still often made the non-resident parent by force. For in most cases of separation it is the father who is forced to leave his home. If the mother does leave nearly always her children are taken with her. This process is enforced on the ground by all sorts of agents, including the police and social services. When this situation is presented in court a locked-out father faces a legal presumption that not living with his children is the status quo. Here the court hides behind the No Order Principle, or CA 1989 section 1(5), which says:

"**Where a court is considering whether or not to make one or more orders under this Act with respect to a child, it shall not make the order or any of the orders unless it considers that doing so would be better for the child than making no order at all.**"

Given this law, the argument goes that an order changing residence, or the level of contact, is something a court cannot know is best for the child or children until evidence is seen, (something that will not happen until the final hearing). Therefore, a father once again finds himself the contact parent at the start of proceedings (which can last a life-changing amount of time for a child), and is thus likely to remain so until the end and beyond the court case. The father is, in effect, faced with trying to argue from the start why he isn't, or shouldn't be, the contact parent.

The law that makes the above situation into an even more grotesque, inhuman travesty is contained in two sections of CA 1989 Section 1(2A):

"... unless the contrary is shown, that involvement of that parent in the life of the child concerned will further the child's welfare."

In subsection (2B):

"...involvement means involvement of some kind, either direct or indirect, but not any particular division of a child's time."

What these sections are unbelievably saying is that the law considers the benefit to a child of being brought up by a natural parent can be reduced to 'indirect contact', meaning as little as a letter once a year. The duplicity of this wording, that Lady Hale managed to get into the Law Act, opened wide the door for abuse of fathers. For, without 'any particular division of time' needed for an order to be legal, and with 'indirect contact' being 'involvement' in a child's life, a Judge has latitude to argue anything meets the needs of a child to be involved with a contact parent, (however that person is labelled).

In its extreme this open-door abuse was merciless on a tidal wave of fathers who came to court with children born out of wedlock between the period 1990 and 2002, and unknowingly without a PR Agreement. With the words from that famous song, *Who's Sorry Now?* [Francis, Connie MGM records, (1958)] ringing in my mind, I witness countless courts dish out No Contact Orders to disbelieving fathers and smiling single-mums. Even today, a father without PR, for example one who did not marry and whose partner did not register him on his child's birth certificate, can still expect only a letter once a year, to or from his offspring, if the mother so insists.

For fathers with PR, prospects under the CA 1989 are better but not good. For what courts typically deem prudent, and nobody knows why, is that the time a resident-parent spends with her children during the school or working week does not count. I guess it is assumed that children come home from school and are fed and watered by the nanny or butler and the mother arrives just as they are being put to bed? For whatever reason, Family Courts only divide up the weekends and school holidays between parents. Presumably, this is seen as the time family members can mix in fun-filled, quality-time – as things like house maintenance, shopping, bill paying and other activities that usually occupy this time should be done by the housekeeper.

Anyone who is not living some sort of wealthy or Victorian existence, and is a normal human being, knows family bonding and parenting of children actually happens during the mundane time. In the living with, sleeping nearby, eating together, or sitting staring at the telly. Yet, none of this is recognised by the Family Courts. As a result, the best possible outcome for a non-resident parent, normally meaning a father, is 20 per cent of time outside of school, i.e. every other weekend and half the school holidays. From this starting point (for an angel of a dad), a resistant mother can argue things down. The average allowance for a contact parent to have with a child in an arrangement ordered by the Family Courts is reliably speculated to be just seven per cent of non-school time.

Yet, it gets worse. Firstly, while there are restrictions on both parents, subject to a child arrangement order, taking their children out of the country for more than 28 days, or moving their child permanently abroad, it is legal for a resident parent to move a child's location within the UK without the permission of the court or the contact parent. More importantly, the use of contact and resident parent distinction has spread throughout society including benefit agencies, police, schools, social care, passport office officials, border control, as well as in the NHS with doctors and nurses. Things you thought you had a right to, like receiving everything from a school the mother receives, suddenly become a matter of pleading and arranging on an individual basis.

Schools often become a bugbear, as unknown to most parents the legal obligations of a school to provide information on their child are, in law, limited. The research I undertook with the Department of Education in Whitehall indicated that the only legal requirement of a school towards any legal guardian was to give one report a year. Of course, the resident parent gets a lot more: invites to plays, information on school trips, copies of school photos, automatic invites to parent evenings and such other things. Yet, as a non-resident parent, you are not legally entitled to any of this, unless you make special arrangements. The unofficial policy of most schools seems to be that they will make provision for a non-resident parent to be given a lot of (but certainly not all) information unless the resident parent objects explicitly, or if the non-resident parent makes a pest of himself.

An example of the above was a case where a resident mother had won one of the infamous No Contact orders against a father. His only source of information on his daughter then came from the mother, in a court-ordered report that was supposed to be sent twice a year, with a photo to be sent once a year, and from school reports and school photos, usually sent twice a year. Once this man's child turned 15-years-old he found all information was cut off bar the one statutory school report, and no one would explain this action. An application by the father for enforcement of the Court Order was put on the back-burner in the courts, and after nine months or so I advised direct action using private investigators. What transpired was that the daughter had gotten pregnant shortly after turning 15-years-old.

This cover-up of the daughter's condition by the school was insisted on by the resident mother, and the school felt they had no choice but to comply. Social services and the court both conspired to delay news reaching the father so he could not use the teenage pregnancy as evidence in another application, being the outcome the father had always earnestly warned in four, full court cases in the Family Court across 12 years. The cover-up worked, as by the time the father found out all the facts his daughter was no longer of an age to be dealt with in the Family Courts, or in any other court.

The impact of contact and resident parent status goes to so many things, more things than I have room to write about, and is everywhere in UK society. When I wrote, 'You cannot beat the Family Courts', this is what I meant. The CA 1989 makes a father a non-resident parent by default, and from then on he is a second-class parent in the eyes of most of those who can affect his family life. Regardless of the exact words used in the Law Act, court processes by their very nature anyway work towards making one party the winner. Only one of the parents in any CAP court case will be the person with whom a child spends the majority of his or her time. However, the extent of defeat can be a shock for anyone who knows the slightest thing about parenting.

THE PARAMOUNTCY PRINCIPLE – AKA THE RIGHT TO BE A CRUEL F**K

The Statutory Law in CA 1989 and Family Practice Directions have at their core, something that on the surface sounds reasonable. The welfare of the child is paramount in all decisions of the Family Court, i.e. CA 1989 section 1 (1):

"When a court determines any question with respect to — (a) the upbringing of a child; or (b) the administration of a child's property or the application of any income arising from it, the child's welfare shall be the court's paramount consideration."

The Paramountcy Principle is a combination of the doctrine of Paramountcy, which is the need to reconcile conflicting laws, (for example, National State laws and County By-laws, on the same matter), and the Welfare Principle, which is that the interests of a child are the essential consideration in all decisions. It is meant to prevent a Dickensian Oliver Twist-like scenario, where the interests of an adult world supersede the welfare of children.

This principle is good enough in the rare case of a father directly abusing his child, who, when his child is taken from him, becomes distraught with grief at the loss. Yet, in the situation where a mother exploits this legal connection between the interests of a child and her wishes, such a mother merely has to insist that any arrangement other than the one she wants would damage her and the court is bound to agree, and with no regard to the father.

Worse still, a Family Court can never be held to account for the suffering it inflicts on a father. Not only is this true under the law used in child arrangements and custody disputes, but it is also true under the UK's Human Rights Act 1998. For although this latter Act forces Judges to adopt the European Convention on Human Rights in their judgments, (including Article Six, the right to a fair trial, and Article Eight, the right to a private and family life), the Act also says that Primary Legislation of the UK takes precedence over the Convention. In other words, while the prejudice of the Family Courts may undermine a father's rights under the European Convention on Human Rights, it is nevertheless lawful for a Family Court Judge to do this because of the Paramountcy Principle. No higher court of review or appeal in the UK would find otherwise.

The agonising torture that a father suffers from losing all contact with his children through a Family Court 'No Contact' order is very hard to relate. The closest analogy I can think of is having your children kidnapped. If a child is killed, you will grieve terribly, and I do not seek to diminish the depth of that grief. However, there is an end to the event of dying, although the loss will stay with you all your life, albeit of fading intensity. In the case of a child kidnap, there is no end to the intensity of loss **and** the grief stays with you, like a death, for the rest of your life. The urgency and immediacy of suffering is never-ending. What is more, if and when you finally do see your children, they will be like zombies, your children but possessed of a spiteful spirit. The child you loved with all your soul will be gone, and in their body a person who does not know you and even hates you.

More bearable than a No Contact Family Court Order is one that gives visitation contact, which consents to a father having a pitifully small amount of time with his offspring such as alternate weekends and half the school holidays. Yet, even in this scenario, a father can be but a condemned man, doomed to watch his kids drift away before they become adults. For without adequate time to be a parent, children become strangers, and in the end will not even want to spend with their father that time a court has allocated.

When the true dreadfulness of a Family Court Order hits home, father-clients of mine often turn to me and ask: "How can he [the Judge] live with himself?"

In these situations, I am always reminded of a social psychology experiment on disassociate thinking. In an American University members of the public were duped into taking part in what they thought was academic research into learning theory. At first, the subjects were inundated with a talk on the importance of the University, the authority of the researchers and so on. The subjects were then told how they were an important part of the programme and were asked to give an electric shock to a man, (who unknown to them was an actor), every time he got a memory-test answer wrong. The catch was that they had to increase the severity of the shock each time a wrong answer was given. In conclusion, the actor would fake extreme pain and then death. Unbelievably 60 per cent of the subjects carried on until the actor had apparently died. The experiment was so shattering in its findings that it has been repeated many times since, but with the same results.

The explanation of this behaviour, and for this experiment it applied more to men than women, is that deferential instincts allow us to disassociate from our actions, under the right conditions. It is what people believe enabled guards in Nazi concentration camps to be both normal people and the perpetrators of genocide. As I have said before, we are both human animals and human beings – Judges no less.

Given this side of human nature, one can rest assured that those who pass the thousands of inhuman orders in the UK's Family Courts have no conscience about what they do. Thanks in part to tricks of the mind like the 'Paramountcy Principle' (aimed at a mythical Dickensian world populated by brutes for fathers and hapless women for mothers) they would say it is what is expected of Judges, or even demanded of them. Condemning good fathers to the sort of punishment society would not inflict on the most terrible of criminals, and without a fair trial, is all in a day's work. Afterwards, I am sure not one of them ever has a twinge of guilt as they go home to their own families.

8

Setting the Context II – Misandrist Misuse of CDA (Claims of Domestic Abuse)

Accusing a man of the physical or sexual mistreatment of a woman is an all-powerful tool at the centre of a lot of modern-day societal injustice. False allegations against men became an epidemic in the UK Family Courts in the 1990s, and are now a pandemic through the #MeToo virtual campaign that attacks high-profile men of wealth or importance. Today, any public agency that might be involved in a family break-up will look for Claims of Domestic Abuse (CDA) like a coiled-spring.

For example, a domestic argument, which spills into someone calling the police, immediately requires that CDA be treated as true until proven false. Attending police will typically include a female officer trained to encourage/help CDA to be made by a woman in the incident. Meanwhile male officers are instructed to try and move the man in the dispute out of his home, on the spot if at all possible. They often use something called a Police Notice that restricts a father from returning to his house (if he hasn't been living there for a while). Social workers from a Local Authority who become involved with a family are also hypersensitive to CDA towards children or mothers, even when denied by both parents. They are also empowered to use subjective methods to pre-judge CDA on the side of caution, before a Family Court has a contested hearing, and record this assessment in a report to a Family Law Judge who then invariably follows their advice.

This widespread sensitivity to CDA is a product of a perceived high-prevalence of violent or sexual abuse in families in general. This perception (of domestic abuse being common in a lot of families) has become a crucial and centre-stage issue in Family Court thinking. As a result, it has also been subjected to a lot of propaganda by feminist-extremists who are against shared-parenting after family bust-ups.

Of course, domestic abuse does genuinely happen. However, the frequency it occurs is highly debatable – something feminists dislike you saying, often labelling you a 'domestic abuse denier' if you do. However, ONS (Office for National Statistics) figures of the number of families in the UK (19 million as of 2018) (10) compared to the number of convictions for domestic abuse by the police (67,000 in 2019) (11) shows that the annual rate of domestic abuse is only 0.35 per cent of all families in the country. Even this figure may be an overestimate as there are distortions. For example, the vast majority of CPS convictions (70 per cent) are consent agreements, meaning a person copped-a-plea before anyone had a chance to weigh an allegation in a legal process. What is more, one-third of domestic abuse victims are men (11).

If we want some measure of the ratio of true to false allegations of domestic abuse, you could reasonably compare the number of crimes where CDA was recorded as being involved, to the number of convictions for domestic abuse, (including those convictions where an agreement was made without a trial). This comparison says only 11 per cent of

CDA are genuine (67,000 out of about 600,000 CDA), (11) although it could be further assumed that the forum of a Family Court creates a greater number of false allegations, as opposed to situations involving the police – so that percentage could in reality be much lower.

Others would strenuously disagree with all of this analysis. Some claim that 90 per cent of **all** children witness, during their time as a child, at least one incident of domestic abuse. Others bandy about all sorts of rehashed-statistics, including that one in four, or 25 per cent of all mothers, are regularly abused by their partner. This confused state of affairs is made murkier by how you define domestic abuse. For what can surprise fathers in Family Court cases is that women's support organisations have helped move its definition-in-law far away from common sense. As an example, one client of mine had a case where the court deliberated on whether standing in front of the TV while his partner was watching a programme, and hiding a kettle in his garden shed, constituted a sufficient domestic abuse for him to be forbidden from living with his children.

GYNOCENTRIC CDA AND FREE LEGAL TEAMS

Since 2014, Legal Aid is no longer available for Child Arrangement Disputes **unless** you can claim you, or your child/children, are the victims of domestic abuse or violence by the other parent.

The powers that be say that either parent can claim domestic abuse by the other parent and get funding. I have even seen on TV earnest-looking women talking about the need to include men as victims of domestic abuse. Without pre-empting the next chapters, I think if we are honest, we all know this is a lie. Sometimes the authorities' attempts to assert treatment of family abuse as gender-blind become comical. For example, if you look at the supposedly unisex list of things a person can bring to claim domestic abuse you will see one of them is a letter from a domestic-abuse shelter saying they were turned away or lived there for 24 hours. Given that there are no domestic-abuse shelters or refuges for men in existence, this is not something a man can get – now is it?

I should make it clear that I am here talking about the Legal Aid Agency's decisions to give funding. The police are well-aware that women can be just as nasty and violent as men, with many injunctions, non-molestation and non-harassment orders being made against women, to protect men. I agree that the abusive nature of women towards children is also known, with 54 per cent of perpetrators being women (12). Yet, when it comes to CDA used in Family Courts, the Legal Aid Agency primarily views abuse as something done by a man to a woman, or even a child. You can call this blind, feminist-inspired, gender-prejudice, and I am sure this is sometimes employed. However, there is also a type of logic I call 'rational prejudice'. This reasoning starts with the assertion that the primary concern of the State is the safety of children. If we also accept that after the separation of parents children nearly always live with their mother until things are sorted out then there is a reasoning that goes like this:

1). If the State funds a Private Law case for a father in which he claims a mother is abusive or neglectful of her children, then it is caught in a Catch-22. For this funding says the mother may be abusing her children during the trial, but at the same time the State is complicit in the crime as it is doing nothing about it. 2). If the State funds a mother over claims of child abuse by their father then the State is safe in saying that this case may not be serious enough for Public or Criminal Law, but it may be that the father is anyway abusing his children. So while a court case proceeds a mother can protect her children as out-of-court-mechanisms in society enable a mother to enforce no contact, if she so chooses. Such State funding of this situation is, therefore, benign. 3). If the State funds a father because he was, or is, being domestically abused by his partner or wife, with whom the children inevitably reside, this can be seen as a misuse of funds as that is not a matter for the Family Courts, which are only concerned with children. However, 4) if a mother accuses her partner of domestic abuse of her that is also abuse of her children, as they live with her, and therefore argument 2) applies.

I have experienced a case that proved this logic. A prospective client was an ethnic Indian who had a son by a wife, brought over from India, in an arranged marriage to which she and he both equally consented. He was a taxi driver on about £17,000 pa, and they lived in a studio apartment. His wife did not initially work, but studied computer programming in evening classes while her husband cared for their child after school. The wife then landed a job, as a result of her study, on a salary of £60,000 pa at which point she left to set up on her own as an independent woman in a flat she bought for herself, apparently abandoning her husband and child. Because the father was a working single-dad social services were deeply involved. They satisfied themselves that the mother had rejected her child, almost from birth, and that the father should be the resident parent of his son.

After a while, the mother's attitude changed and she applied to have joint care of her son. The father applied for Legal Aid for the ensuing Child Arrangement Dispute. He claimed he had been abused, because the mother had thrown a dirty laundry basket at him, and she had abused her son by one time undressing in front of him. Despite the flimsiness of these allegations they were accepted as a cause for the father being granted Legal Aid. As a consequence, he won his case and the mother was given only supervised contact with her child once a month.

What this demonstrates is the underlying logic given in the preceding paragraphs that the Legal Aid Agency can take sides, but based on who is the resident parent, not the gender of the parent.

I know this case history is a rare example, and I know it does not address the issue of fathers forcibly being made the non-resident parent. However, it is nevertheless instructive of 'rational prejudice': a process that holds to a few precepts that favour one sex, but is otherwise rational. This chink in the Family Court process should give a father hope, and to this I will return in chapter 10.

Legal Aid rules, LASPO and CDA

The agency that decides if someone qualifies to have the State pay their legal team's bills is called the Legal Aid Agency. If the State is going to pay someone's lawyers, that person has to have a full legal team, and the key is the solicitor. Every solicitor who offers Legal Aid is allocated a set amount of work, (like milk quotas). So any Legal Aid applicant must first contact solicitors registered under the Legal Aid scheme and ask if they have any availability to take on new clients. If the answer is yes, an applicant will then have to meet the criteria set by the agency to get funding for each different type of work.

Most State funding requires applicants to pass a 'means and merits test'. Firstly, an applicant has to have limited financial means of his own (normally an income below a certain threshold, and savings below a certain amount – **See Appendix IV for a tool that will help you with seeing if this applies to you**). Also, the case they want to pursue or defend has to have enough merit (as judged by their barrister or solicitor, and a Legal Aid Agency adjudicator), meaning a good chance of being successful.

Do not assume that a person cannot get aid because they are working. Even if income rules them out, they may qualify for legal aid with a small contribution towards it. The rules on income are relaxed for applications for protective injunctions, and some sorts of cases attract funding without a means and merits test requirement.

It used to be that to claim State funding of lawyers because of domestic abuse, a woman had to produce documents to show her claims were genuine, and these documents had to be no more than a year old, and usually from the police. Things have moved on. For the funding of Private Law cases in Family Courts, domestic abuse is now defined in the guidance document: *The Legal Aid, Sentencing and Punishment of Offenders Act (LASPO) 2012 – Evidence Requirements for Private Family Law Matters*; last review date January 2018, and the Law Act behind this funding, i.e. LASPO. Within this guide, the age of documents that can be used has increased from one to five years old, and there is talk of it being extended to any time in the past. Also, the list of evidence a woman can now use to claim Legal Aid because of domestic abuse has become extensive. Only one of the following documents is needed:

a. A copy of a relevant conviction, or a caution, or ongoing criminal proceedings, for domestic violence against the applicant for Legal Aid, by the other party. For convictions, an applicant can rely on an unspent conviction, regardless of how long ago it occurred, but spent convictions have to be within the last five years. Ongoing proceedings should only be used if the other party has been charged.

b. A copy of a relevant protective injunction, protective order, binding over order, or protective notice against the other party to protect the applicant from domestic violence. Even if an injunction was discharged, it still counts as long as it was first granted less than five years before the court case.

c. A copy of an undertaking (e.g. not to harass or go near the other party) such as made within a court case or at a police station. Importantly an undertaking cannot be used as evidence if the applicant for Legal Aid gave a cross-undertaking (i.e. agreed not to do the same thing).

d. Evidence that the other party is on police bail for a relevant domestic abuse offence against the applicant. This evidence ends once bail ends.

e. A letter from a member of MARAC (Multi-Agency Risk Assessment Conference) confirming the applicant for Legal Aid was referred to in a conference, as a victim of domestic violence and that the conference put in place a plan to protect that person from a risk of harm by the other party in the case.

f. A copy of a UK Court Finding of Facts, that there has been domestic violence by the other party.

g. A letter or report from a health professional, such as your GP, community psychiatric nurse, midwife, (a little tricky for a father) or health visitor. The letter must confirm that they have examined you within the last five years and found injuries or conditions consistent with being a victim of domestic violence and that they have no reason to believe this was not caused by domestic violence. The person has to have had full access to all your medical records.

h. A letter from a branch of UK social services, confirming an assessment, or a copy of the assessment, in which you were a victim of domestic abuse, or were considered at risk of such.

i. A letter from a domestic violence support organisation that you spent 24 hours or more in a domestic violence refuge, or that you were turned away from it because it was full.

j. Evidence of financial abuse (since 2016) based on either a statement, diary entries, a letter from a domestic support organisation, text messages, emails, evidence from credit cards and bank statements.

NB: Most documents must not be more than five years old, from the date of the application to the Legal Aid Agency **and** from the date of the event on the document. Documents must give dates, and name the applicant as the victim, i.e. despite Clare's Law offences against someone else are not supposed to count. Lists of what is a relevant domestic or child abuse criminal offence can be found on the Gov.uk website, details of which are in **Appendix IV**. Whether or not a conviction is spent or unspent can be determined on the 'Your Rights' website.

Also, a parent can claim Legal Aid because of child abuse by the other party. Unlike the treatment of documents proving domestic abuse of a partner, child abuse documents can only be a maximum of two years old, but can relate to any child and not necessarily the child or children in the Family Court case for which aid is being sought. The sorts of documents needed in these situations are:

1) A copy of a relevant conviction, or caution, or ongoing criminal proceedings for a child abuse offence. Unspent convictions apply regardless of how long ago the offence was, otherwise it must not be more than two years ago. Ongoing proceedings must involve the other party having been charged.
2) A protective injunction against the other person made to protect the child in the case, either still in force or made within the last two years.
3) A copy of a fact-finding made in proceedings in the UK at some point in the last two years, saying that the other parent abused a child.
4) Evidence of the other person being on bail for abuse of any child.
5) A letter from social services, confirming that at some point in the last two years there was a child protection plan in place to protect the child in this case from abuse by the other party, or that the other party had been assessed as having abused the child in the case, or had been assessed as being at risk of abusing the child.
6) An application for a protective injunction made at the same time as the application for a Family Court Order for a children arrangements order, which has not yet been dealt with.

I would defy any mother who hasn't been a victim of domestic abuse **not** to be able to provide one of the proofs mentioned for abuse of a partner. For instance, all a mother has to do is convince other women in social services, or MARAC, or her female health visitor, or some female nurse or midwife, that she is sometimes a little frightened of her husband and then really, it's job done! A devious woman could invent injuries and get a GP, or nurse, to sign a letter without the other party ever knowing, or make a false statement that she was financially abused, or turn up at a woman's sanctuary when she knows it's full. More commonly women seeking to 'game the system', by getting this free legal help, just manufacture an incident to kick things off – and a typical ploy is reneging on arrangements with a father to see his children, so sending him into a rage.

When LASPO laws came into effect in 2013, statistics showed a massive effect on the justice families and children got dealt as a result. The group of people where both parties had legal teams in Private Law, Family Court cases went down 25 percentage points, from 2012 to 2017, with a consequential rise of cases with only one party having legal representation. In other words, the inequality of funding took hold as thousands of fathers overnight found themselves without a legal team, while their ex's kept, or obtained, help. What is more, while court cases in the Family Courts initially dropped, they have since risen to their previous levels, only now with enhanced injustice.

Having a free legal team is an enormous advantage, something that lawyers and Judges refuse to acknowledge. Yet, for an ordinary bloke, the psychological drain of going through a court process is made so much worse by the knowledge that he is also draining his life savings for an uncertain outcome. At the same time, the chances of a woman being penalised for perjury over false CDA are minimal to non-existent.

The widespread misuse of CDA is self-evident in all statistical analysis. For example, the number of non-molestation orders issued in 2013, the year Legal Aid was cut for Family Court applications, jumped 18 per cent nationwide, and in one area of the UK these figures showed an immediate 90 per cent increase in 2013, (13). Furthermore, since 2013, the number of Private Law Cases involving domestic abuse has suddenly started to precisely track the number of Child Arrangement Dispute Cases, at about the 10-13 per cent level, or around 5,000 cases each year (1).

It is not as if those in the court system are blind to the misuse of CDA, or can even claim they disagree with the figures. Sir James Munby made the following comment at the Families Need Fathers Conference in March 2017:

"We know that people game the system, and the classic example of that is one of the bits of LASPO is you do get Legal Aid if there's an allegation of domestic violence."

Rather than address this persecution of fathers, Parliament, (now festooned with women MPs elected to female-candidate-only seats), have passed bills to widen this definition even further. It is now easier to talk about what isn't, rather than what is, domestic abuse. This is where we find ourselves as fathers in 21st Century Great Britain.

CDA TO PRE-EMPT COURT ORDERS

Civil injunctions are in general expensive and challenging to get. However, Family Court injunctions are relatively easy to obtain. The 1996 Family Law Act, along with the Child Support Act, was meant to help the State shift the burden of supporting lone mothers onto fathers. Part IV of this Act deals with kicking fathers out of their house, their main lifetime asset, as part of a divorce – called an occupation order, or notice to vacate. This Law Act also gives a mechanism for a mother to get an injunction to stop fathers venting their anger at losing, namely a non-molestation order, or non-harassment order.

However, these legal tools are now being widely used to gain the upper hand in child arrangement disputes. For it became apparent to many that who it is that wins a child arrangement dispute is often who has residence of the children in a dispute, at the start of proceedings. Fathers, therefore, started to stage sit-ins, in a safe-room within their homes, until child arrangements had been finalised. This father-strategy can be undone by the use of form FL401, which is an application to the Family Courts for a protective injunction based on alleged domestic abuse. It is most effective when made immediately before, or at the same time as, defending or applying for a Section 8 CA 1989 Order.

An FL401 application can give a mother Legal Aid without the need to convince the CPS to prosecute a father. There is little in the Family Law Act 1996 Part IV, e.g. sections 42 and 42A, by way of guidance for a Family Court on when **not to** make an order under this Law, and neither in the relevant Family Practice Directions Part 10. Yet, there are reams of advice in Family Practice Direction 12J defining domestic abuse widely, to encompass almost any behaviour.

Such injunctions can be applied for in the same Family Courts that run child arrangements, and cases can be held within a week of an FL401 form being sent, via an ex-party hearing, without notice to the other side. Thanks to new Practice Directions in the CAP process and unofficial Judge Study Board directives, decisions on such applications err on the side of caution for the applicant, and injustice for an accused. Being all about domestic abuse, these applications can be both self-financing and self-fulfilling. For once an injunction is given, usually by a Judge different from the CAP case Judge, the tone of hearings is set and the father appears guilty from the outset.

Apart from fast-tracking a CAP court case towards the conclusion a mother wants, injunctions can also reduce fathers to quivering wrecks. Although these orders are under Civil Law, they can have a power of arrest attached, and a Family Court has the power to inflict significant sanctions on a father who breaks these orders, including time in prison.

In one case, a client of mine became frantic about facing a Family Court for breaching a Go Notice. He had reached across the threshold of his prior home into a porch to unhook his children's raincoats when he picked them up. Significantly, this had involved him placing a foot inside the house, for which the wife wanted him sent to prison. However, I pointed out that enforcement of such injunctions is the responsibility of the applicant in whose name the injunction is in favour. While a father may be arrested for breaching a Family Court injunction, as a way of removing him from the situation, it is the person who has the order that must bring a case to court for a sanction, **and not the CPS.** Typically in this situation, the accused **will not go to prison** on remand, but if arrested, will be released on police bail pending the outcome of a Family Court trial, (if such occurs at all).

Injunctions under the Family Act 1996 can last from one year up to the time the last child in a family reaches 18 years old. These injunctions can be made by consent — but don't do this, however much your children are held to ransom — and are different from Undertakings (especially Mutual Undertakings).

CDA AND FACT-FINDING HEARINGS

Once you get into the Child Arrangement Programme (CAP) at court, even if CDA has not been raised at all before, and even if the other party did not fill in a C1A form, there is still an opportunity to use it and invoke a Fact-Finding Hearing. Although in theory, a court can use a Fact-Finding to determine any unclear facts relevant to a decision about child arrangements, and not just to determine the truth of CDA.

Speeding of a case straight to a Fact Finding is usually a sure signal to a father that a court is railroading him, as the purpose of this hearing is nearly always the same – to enshrine CDA against a father as legal facts. **This is one of the main ways that fathers lose their children** as it is nearly always a precursor to a No Contact Order, should one be in the offing. As a father, I would resist this type of hearing at all costs. One way is to insist on further hearings to add in or limit down the content of the Fact-Finding Hearing bundle.

In Fact-Finding Hearings no oversight exists at all of a Family Court Judge's sole opinion as to which of the two accounts of private, undocumented, and unrecorded family-life is true or false. What is more, there is no burden of proof needed to make a legal decision, no evidence required, as in a criminal case, and the facts found as true **cannot be**

appealed in any UK court, ever. The only hope for a father, once false facts are made legally true, is that procedural rules within that hearing were not adhered to sufficiently to make an appeal possible, and so force the dismissal of the hearing's findings.

After a Fact-Finding Hearing a father or mother can be directed to attend further assessments, other than with social workers, to determine their motives for things they were found to have done – primarily to determine if their application to the court is itself domestic abuse, i.e. brought out of malice rather than a desire to see their children. In this, a party should not be **required** to undergo a psychiatric or medical assessment or treatment. However, Practice Direction 12J, Section 11, allows a court to make any proposed child arrangement or Contact Order conditional on such activities, by consent. Fathers often leap at this as a last chance to vindicate themselves from the false findings made by a court. Yet, make no mistake, such Directions are a trap. However confident you are in your sanity and your just cause, under scrutiny no one survives a psychological or psychiatric assessment when the expert has been told you have done bad things — you did not do — and where the assessor is not allowed to even consider in his analysis that the facts found by a court may actually be wrong.

Works cited, but not referenced in the text

10. **Knipe, Emily.** *Families and Households: 2017.* [ONS, 8th November, 2017].
11. **Elkin, Meghan.** *Domestic Abuse in England and Wales, in the year ending March, 2018.* [ONS, 22nd November, 2018].
12. *Child Maltreatment 2015.* [U.S. Department of Health & Human Services].
13. *Analysis of Post LASPO Use of Non-Molestation Orders.* [FNF Analysis, 15th October, 2018].
1. *Family Court Statistics Quarterly, England and Wales, Annual,* 2017 *(including October to December 2017).* [Ministry of Justice, 2018].

9

Setting the Context III – Gynocentric Assumptions & Practices in the Family Courts

The organisation FNF (Families Need Fathers) believes that what is needed to stop injustice for fathers in the Family Courts is a change in the Children Act 1989 that says that there should be a 'presumption of shared residence', for all Section 8 Orders. Yes, this would help, although the parts of the same Act mentioned in chapter seven would also need to be changed for there to be any hope of equality between biological mothers and fathers in court. However, you will not find the real justification for side-lining fathers en masse in the words of the law or Court Directives, neither of which, currently anyway, enter into a distinction of resident and contact parent.

There are McKenzie Friends that are insistent that cases can be won by careful use of the words of the law, through legal argument introduced via 'points of law'. Point of law is where a barrister in a hearing asks for a ruling on a part of the law affecting a case. All other parties, the father (if represented by a barrister) and the mother and social workers have to leave the court as the professionals pour over the meaning of the words in any part of a Law Act or Court Practice Directive. At the end of this process, the Judge rules on what he will take as the meaning in his hearing. If the barrister who has called for a point of law disagrees with the Judge, he can ask for a 'written legal ruling' at which point the Judge can adjourn while he goes and writes out his reasoning. The purpose of this performance is first, to get accepted into a case part of a legal argument that someone intends to use and secondly, if the meaning of the point of law is wrongly interpreted this flaw can then be used as a basis of an appeal. In practice, Lower Court Judges are not easily bent to being constrained in this way. Often they will simply not give ground to a call for a point of law, or simply ignore it even if they do rule on it. Also, even if a Judge fails to tiptoe through the restrictions of law, and an appeal is subsequently granted, points of law are not all there is to an appeal case, and even if you nevertheless win an appeal it can still be a defeat for a father (see chapter 14).

Other McKenzie Friends recommend that sound research in Case Law can uncover precedents that can win a case. Or that a well-crafted position statement, or some other preliminary document, can be a winning factor. In practice, the Case Law approach suffers from the same faults as 'points of law', and a few others besides, and a position statement is just a briefing document for a court, and does not have prime importance.

Yet other McKenzies, as well as the Judiciary's initiative for 'transparency in the law', say that the answer for fathers in countering any perceived bias in the Family Courts is to fight their corner with a better understanding of court processes, so as not to trip themselves up. A lot of McKenzie Friend advice can come under this heading, often telling fathers it is all their fault courts are biased as they have the wrong attitude. It is indeed no use at all, in the midst of a Family Court case, to hit upon the realisation that justice in the UK is other than you thought. Yet, to blame a victim of bias for that bias is obviously wrong.

THE REAL REASON FOR BEING MADE A NON-RESIDENT PARENT

While all of the above advice has merit, being more finely tuned in the technicalities of advocacy and litigation is not the nub of the problem. All the aforementioned points are tangential. The most significant impact on a Judge's decisions are the 'informal directives' that worm through the whole system of Family Courts like a virus. Inequalities in the law are mere clothes pegs upon which prejudice is hung. As an example, the former Head of the Family Division, Lady Butler-Sloss, is infamously accredited with letting slip a comment during one of her court cases:

"The needs of a child are intrinsically tied to the needs of the mother."

Although this aside has never been exactly verified, it is nonetheless a reliable insight into the minds of those who decide whether you get to keep your children. Totally verified is the quote by the subsequent Head of the Family Courts for England and Wales, Sir Mark Potter, (provided in chapter two of this book). To reiterate what he said about the rulings of all Family Courts in the UK during his time:

"... The mother, therefore, held all the cards in the court proceedings. The absolute priority of the courts was to foster the best possible relationships for the child with both parents, but the rulings of the court rebounded badly on fathers. I would have to accept that the dice were all loaded against fathers."

This admission spotlights what drives the machinery of Lower Courts so evidently working against a father, regardless of what a father says, does, or how a father is represented, and what points of law or Case Histories are raised. As a direct import of this top-down direction, a whole bunch of misandrist axioms are now held by Judges throughout the UK; some spoken and some not, e.g:

a) Shared-parenting, meaning children having two homes following the separation of their parents, is unworkable and harmful to children.
b) Hostility to the mother is an abuse of the child.
c) Allegations of domestic abuse are no less credible because they were not made at the time of the alleged event, or because they are spoken about for the first time when they give an advantage to a mother in court.
d) Parent alienation as a process does not exist.
e) Separating children from fathers while a court case is ongoing has no long-term effect on a father-child relationship.
f) Children separated completely from their father will seek him out after they are 18 years old, and re-bond if the father is any good.
g) A child's true wishes are always faithfully expressed in a court through social service staff.

Such bias thinking avoids scrutiny because Family Court cases are held in secret. This condition of confidentiality on Family Court hearings means no outside observers, no law students or solicitor interns sitting on the back row of the public benches taking notes. Injustice resting on the above precepts can be dished out quite openly.

To beat the system of Family Courts a father needs not only to address the opposing case, (which he has to understand as well as his own), but he also needs to understand and address these unspoken, unwritten prejudices as well, or risk going off on a destructive tangent of defeat (see chapter 12).

HOW DID IT COME TO THIS?

This question is what most men ask, with moistening eyes, at the end of a typical Family Court case after being stripped of their God-given right to bring up their children. It is a question that, surprisingly, I have never heard answered. When you are living in times of gender-discrimination denial, when society at large is saying the very opposite of what is going on, it is hard to identify the mechanisms and reasons why a system against fathers came into being. I believe even those who are today elaborating the processes of discrimination against fathers do not themselves understand why they are allowed to get away with so much blatant sexism.

Like others, I am mystified how such a society-injustice has come to be the accepted and legal norm. Yet, it is a question that deserves an answer. What I can do is offer some speculation, even though many will see this as conspiracy-theory nonsense. Upfront, I can say that to me the fulcrum of change was the rise of single mothers, and the pivotal point in time the 1970s.

Let me split the main question into two: 1. why has discrimination against fathers come into being? and 2. what are the mechanisms that changed the law to allow it?

Dealing with the why, we all know it is an inescapable part of the human condition that men and women want and have sex with each other. Before the invention of the birth control pill in the 1960s there was little that constrained this basic animal instinct from bringing forth children, (despite the best efforts of Marie Stopes and the invention of early latex condoms — the latter of which mostly just made prostitution less hazardous). Childbearing, the creation of families, by its very nature forces men and women into dependent roles, roles which suppressed the free will of both genders, equally.

In the Industrial Revolution World of the 1800s to early 1900s, the average working man was condemned by his natural predilection to a lifetime of endless and thankless toil, to support a mostly economically inactive partner and his children (that is when they were not drafted to be blown to bits in nationalist wars). Women were equally shackled, from their late teens to early twenties, to a role as a wife that kept them from much involvement in the world outside of a home until they were in their 30s. Families were held together out of circumstance, love and the need to bring up an average of six children per household.

Up to say 1910, given that nearly everyone rented their homes (save a small 11 per cent), both men and women worked in their respective roles until they dropped dead. Aged, married couples, no longer able to work and therefore able to pay rent (which often was for a house tied to work), rarely lived out their lives together. Often the Grandfather died in some version of a workhouse, breathing his last with strangers all around him, while a Grandmother was taken in by one of her daughters to provide free childcare. Such was the fate of my Great Grandfather and Great Grandmother, both upper working-class average people, brought up close to the epicentre of the world's Industrial Revolution, Glasgow.

In short, in the past men worked until they were about 30, at which point they could afford to take on a wife. Having a wife meant a new baby every 18 months or so, and after you had raised all these children, without time to take a breath, at an average age of 64 years, you died. Law Courts were unaffordable, divorce was rarely allowed, and although marital separations did happen they occurred at a fraction of today's rates and were done in secret.

Britain then had a series of shocks with the mass slaughter of young and able men by a flu pandemic, (that killed mostly men in their early twenties), and World War I. After these events, and connected to them, the right to vote was removed as the exclusive preserve of property-owners and given to everyone. The power of the ballot box then pressed the Government to change the institution of marriage, which resulted in the Matrimonial Causes Act 1937. This Law Act widened the legal reasons a woman could use to divorce her husband to include any one of: desertion, drunkenness or insanity, instead of just adultery and cruelty as before. However, the divorce courts were still inaccessible and unaffordable to most until after WWII, when the processes of divorce were streamlined to help the countless women who found themselves estranged from their husbands. For example, because they were missing in action, but not declared dead, or had chosen not to return from abroad to marital servitude in the UK.

However, although more available, divorce or separation meant, right up to the 1960s, any children of a former union typically went with their father, (or maybe some relative like a Grandparent). As there was no way for women to independently raise their children outside of marriage and finding another man willing to bring up someone else's children was rare. You must also realise that 'children' meant many. Not the average of six you could expect in families of the late 1800s, (with frequent occurrence of families of 10 or more children), but an average of three by 1958, (with one in ten families having over seven).

Across all of the above times unmarried mothers were always outcasts in society, no different to the poor souls you can now see sleeping on our streets in modern Britain. Special orphanages and independent carers took in unwanted children in something called Baby Farming. In one orphanage, for offspring of unmarried mothers in Edinburgh, children were left in a basket nailed to a hatch on a back door. The mother would rotate the basket and the hatch would lock, the mother never to see her child again. Many such infants died of the cold as the matrons collected children in the mornings, whereas unmarried mothers typically scurried to such places at night. It was also a time the UK was still sending unwanted and orphaned children to the British Colonies of Canada and Australia, where they worked as unpaid farm-slaves until they were old enough to escape. All of this happened up to only a decade before the pivotal point of the 1970s.

Change in the lot of a family was needed, and after 1950 that is what we got as a Labour Government constructed a Post-War Welfare State in the UK, something that still emblemises Europe today. Within this was the NHS, social housing (houses for heroes), benefits for those with children, and nationalisation of industries to ensure enough work-for-wages to feed families.

There were, however, unintended consequences of the UK's social revolution when combined with post WWII shifts in responsibilities. Firstly, the job of social work passed from Boards of Guardians to Local Government Authorities, and during the war it went to school teachers for a while. As a result the culture of removing children into homes, or deporting them to the Colonies, fell out of favour. New social housing and benefits enabled Local Authorities to allow lone mothers to care for their children on their own, so that for the first time single-mums could live independently.

Over subsequent decades being a single mother has become a passport to securing a home and future for a family. Even today, although social housing has dried up, living on benefits for mothers is OK (until her children reach 16 years old), especially when combined with the allowed 16 hours-a-week of work. As a consequence the number of single-mum families in the UK climbed from a tiny fraction of one per cent in the 1950s, to 1.8 million or one-quarter of all families with dependent children, in 2014 (18). If we include those families with a step-parent and dependent children, (that is families with a lone mother who has taken another partner), this grouping makes up one-third of all families with dependent children in the country (19). This change in family demographics, in such a very short space of time, speaks of a transformation in the country as a whole.

A second change that impacted family life in Great Britain was wartime legislation for the protection of women in the workplace. In the 1950s this Act was extended to include protection from racial discrimination, as the UK plugged labour-shortages with immigrants from its Colonies. Protection of minorities at work fell under the responsibility of a variety of commissions to do with equal opportunities. Like all such bureaucracies, these commissions acquired more resources, power and influence for their own sake. Yet the issue of equal opportunities found especially fertile ground in the urgent need for a diverse labour force to fuel a post-war revival. Although this driver was sated by the 1970s, when the UK economy crashed into recession, the momentum of the bureaucracy continued and created a new organisation: the infamous Equal Opportunities Commission, (that notably was 75 per cent staffed by women). This commission was backed by a new law: the Sex Discrimination Act 1975.

The Equal Opportunities Commission's work on the rights of women had a smooth ride, as contrary to what modern-day rewrites of history say men were delighted to have more women enter the workforce in the second half of the 1900s. In fact, given a choice most would rather have a female than a male recruit. As a result, the UK's demographics sharply shifted again with women going from 14 per cent of the workforce in 1974, to the present day 49 per cent. Along the way, many consensual marriages, affairs and liaisons developed at work (some high-profile ones now being rewritten under the virtual campaign #MeToo). Today most professional jobs, employment in the media and other well-paid lines of work are all dominated by women, (not least of all Family Law solicitors). Meanwhile, men still dominate the mucky work, the dangerous jobs, the outdoor manual employment (15) – a downtrodden labour force in overalls and fluorescent orange.

When you combine these shifts in demographics with the arrival, in the 1960s, of man-made chemistry to reliably control, (for the first time in humanity's history), female fertility, a complete breakdown in the interdependent roles within families came about. Women can now have sex for fun, or procreation, by choice – and they don't need their partner's permission or knowledge to switch. When children arrive, (and now the average family has less than two children), they can marry the biological father, marry the State, or raise their children by subcontracting motherhood and working full time. And, they can switch between any of these states on a whim. The need to jump from one marriage to another, as was the case up to the 1960s, has gone. Women's 'human condition' is now different. Altered not by a conspiracy of women or anything at all to do with that window-dressing and lies of Women's Lib, but as a result of changes made by men — for the greater good of society — having unintended consequences.

It is this revolution in the human condition for women that created the 'why' of legislation against fathers. For these newly independent women, (independent financially and of their fertility), sought freedom from the one remaining restraint on their family lives, 'the rights of fathers over their children' – of fathers they no longer wanted.

Meanwhile, men have not stopped having sex with women because things are unfair, and so men's human condition remains unaltered. The role of men in society is still a lifetime as a wage-slave, sometimes for themselves, sometimes for a mother of their children, and sometimes for someone else's children, or someone else's ex-wife/partner. Men have become the fly-in-the-ointment of choice, whining about wanting to bring up their children when a woman wants to do as she pleases and opt for life as a single mum, or with a new monogamous partner.

Statistics point to the pivotal point of this change as the 1970s, when, for the first time, divorce courts were inundated with disputes over where children should live after separation. Before this time, if there were disputes at all, they were normally in the opposite direction as parents tried to unload children on each other.

Without going any further, it should now be clear what the answer is to the question: **why**? Why the demand for change. So what about the **how**?

The 'how' can be more mysterious than the why – so secretively are an elite of women in London. It seems to involve an unholy trinity: female control of crucial roles in the Civil Service (also the one), female power in State-owned media, and excessive Government sponsorship of extremist-charities opposed to shared-parenting following divorce or separation.

Ground zero of the 'how' seems to have been the recruitment of women into the workplace in large numbers during WWII. While the vast majority of such jobs were handed back to men after the armies of Europe were demobbed, some key ones were not. Most notably, numbers of Government civil servants in administrative roles rose during the war from around 40,000 non-industrial civil servants (meaning not doing manual work) during the time Britain had an empire across one-quarter of the world's surface, to 400,000 during the war (or 1.2 million including those doing physical work). Previously the domain of a male-public-school-elite, Civil Service administrative departments (including the BBC) became multi-gender, and many of these jobs were kept in an enlarged Labour-controlled Post-War Public Service. This involvement of, and control by, women in the work of public service was a significant transformation of two of the nine pillars-of-governance that run this country, i.e. the Central and Local Civil Service. For, before the war, women were explicitly excluded from employment in the Civil Service as they could at any time have children, leaving departments in the lurch. All of this was swept aside and remains swept.

You should note I said control and not heading-up. Men still dominate top Civil Service jobs (albeit diminishingly). Yet, anyone who has worked in a large organisation will know middle managers actually have all the power and do what they want, paying lip-service to top-down directives (that they anyway control by their ownership of information). Today 54 per cent of all civil servants are female, (70 per cent in some departments) (20), as well as 67 per cent of BBC employees (14). Yet, sexual selection in the workplace is not uniform. So in truth, in key areas within both the BBC and the Civil Service, 'women-only' silos developed long ago.

These single-gender silos of public servants had the potential to meet the pent-up demand of a new demographic of independent women. What was needed was an impetus. For even though departments in the Civil Service may, through the opinion of their most populous gender, be inclined to favour things that benefit women, there needed to be something on which to exercise this bias. For anti-father legislation, there are a couple of historical points I could highlight as setting stones in motion and igniting the whole powder keg. One was the formation of the first Woman's Refuge by Erin Pizzey combined with the Divorce Reform Act 1969, and another, the 1993 formation of the CSA (Child Support Agency) to enforce the Child Support Act 1991.

The Divorce Reform Act 1969 for the first time allowed no-fault divorces, requiring only that the parties to a divorce petition be separated for two years, if a mutual application, or five years if only one applicant. Of course, this new law could only be used if a husband or wife had somewhere to go. Under the shadow of this Act, Erin Pizzey opened her house in 1971, in Hounslow, London, for women wanting to escape their marriage. Wives and children came from all over the country and soon she was accommodating up to 60 people, most of who claimed to have been battered. In her words, there were two types: those who were innocent and accidental victims of a violent partner, and those who were themselves violent and created and sought out violent relationships – which Erin described as at least 60 per cent of visitors. Initially resisted, Erin's shelter started something that for Local Authorities soon became an informal duty: to provide funding for women's sheltered housing.

However, the organisations providing this shelter, by Erin's account, were quickly seized upon by a group of Marxist students, who:

"...were looking for a just cause to takeover, to finance their extreme political views [that there was no place in society for men]." (17).

The interlopers she referred to were part of a movement that had run out of steam, public interest, and funds; the movement which had come from New York: the Women's Liberation Movement. Far from being the root cause of anything, up until this point, Women's Libers were an obscure intellectual group who sought to replace Capitalism with Communism because in the former system women were deemed repressed. It is why we now have the term 'PC' with all it implies about being scared to say something that challenges a view, however crazy. For the Women's Lib movement took from their Marxist roots the philosophy that dissenters cannot be allowed to even speak certain words – but must be eliminated like the committee of pigs did to others in George Orwell's *Animal Farm*.

Erin Pizzey was subjected to this medicine and went into hiding following death threats from Libers who she criticised for using the myth of widespread domestic abuse as an engine for gaining Government funding. With Erin gone, women's refuges soon changed into being Women Refuges **and** Women's Advocacy charities. With the need for shelters for women quite small, Government money nowadays mostly finances successive campaigns for discrimination against men, especially over children. The most active and well-resourced of such organisations are perhaps Refuge and Women's Aid.

With the formation of these charities, a three-cornered plate of corruption was set spinning in the UK. Issues are developed and promoted by extremists in well-heeled charities. These are then fed through personal networks of women to form high-profile news stories run by, primarily, the BBC, and via personal contacts in the branches of the Civil Service involved in drafting legislation. The one-sided publicity of the BBC then generates pressure on elected members of the House of Commons, wishing to satisfy the female vote, just as suggestions for change from the Civil Service appear, giving the elected house a way of meeting an outcry the media has falsely created.

In a nutshell, this is the **how** of discrimination against fathers becoming the norm in this country.

The CSA was a recent gift to this process, thrown up by circumstance. For in the 1980s, the rise of the new demographic of single-mums on benefits was sucking the country's oil-wealth from under Thatcher's feet. To combat this drain the idea was developed to make separated-fathers responsible for the greater part of a lone mother's income, on the threat to the women that they would lose all benefits unless they pointed out their man. Such an 'it's all the fault of dead-beat fathers' stance, of course, came from departments of the Civil

Service manned mostly by women, and backed by a woman Prime Minister. No regard was given to the fact that most single-mums had little connection to the men they had used to get impregnated, and that these men now had other families in traditional relationships to feed. Excuses used by women to avoid this process, knowing that you cannot get blood from a stone and the father of their children would default regardless of the penalty, became famously comical. One reads, "I was being sick out of a window during a party and was unexpectedly taken from behind. I do not know by whom." And another, "... when you eat a can of beans, it is not possible to say which particular bean caused you to fart."

Rewrites of Family Law in the 1980s accompanied the impetus of the CSA and their Law Act, with a skewing of property settlements in divorce cases to the standard split of marital wealth averaging 86:14 in favour of wives, when children are involved (thanks in part to the White vs White case in 1996). These new Laws, in turn, led to a sort of rational-prejudice on child-residence after divorce. For you cannot allow children to be with a father for long when he has been reduced to living in a bedsit. It then follows that for the safety of children, seeing an estranged father for 20 per cent of children's time, makes some sort of sense, even if by so doing those children will gradually become alienated from their father for life.

It has taken 160 years to come to this point following the passing of The Matrimonial Causes Act 1857. This Law Act marked the beginning of intimate Judicial-interference in the family lives of British citizens. It changed marriage from a sacrament ruled by Ecclesiastical Courts, control by the Church, to a contract under Judicial Law, controlled by the State. Under the Church marriage was about a lifelong, monogamous, heterosexual-union for procreation, with the use of contraception a sin (something that the Protestant and Catholic Churches did not part ways on until 1933). Following the shift in power the State initially worked in partnership with the Church, but about 90 years ago it started to strip marriage of all its religious precepts.

Nowadays, marriage is a legal contract between any two people, easy to enter into and easy to leave, with no penalties for breaking the oaths involved. Some — feminists, single-mums, step-parents, homosexuals, polygamous men — may say for the better. Others disagree. For, marriage has also become a one-sided contract when it involves the union of opposite genders. When children are conceived, men must pay a special cancellation fee, which can be an average 86 per cent of a man's entire worldly-wealth and the loss of his offspring. Heterosexual men who seek to avoid this raw-deal by cohabitating, rather than marrying, fare little better. Thanks to the misandrist workings of the CSA Agency and Law, as well as the Family Courts and the Children Act, an unmarried father must provide an income for the mother of his children after he leaves, but he can nevertheless still expect to lose his children if the mother so decides.

Some would say that when Judicial Law deviated the contract of marriage from the principles of the Church it lost a connection to morality and harmony between the sexes. Others would say religious principles of marriage were the very cause of the widespread abuse and subjugation of women. It is a debatable point. Perhaps all that has happened is that the roles the Church prescribed for married-couples have been thrown out, as no longer relevant, but in so doing feminists have seized the momentum to promote women as the superior-sex in family matters. What is undeniable is that **any morality** is greatly tested during the separation of parents with dependent children, however that union was formed. It is also self-evident that there is no point at all in turning to the Civil Courts for help finding morality in such separations, especially in the UK, as our courts have been thoroughly corrupted by a gynocentric, sometimes misandrist, culture that has simply swapped the gender of the victim in families in a retort to what was claimed under the rule of religion.

You can argue however you want, but what history teaches us is that the present-day meddling by the UK's various Family Laws is unstable and destined for failure. For it is well-known, to any student of sociology, that any law requires both force, to implement it, and the acceptance of that law in the hearts of man. Societies were built using these two forces, (with a head of a religion, or philosophical leader, as well as a Regent or dictator). Without both of these mechanisms-of-control the rule of a law will eventually break down.

How change will come for the Family Courts I do not know. Maybe there will be mass disobedience of unjust orders, or a rise in child abductions. Perhaps change will come through the intervention of an outside authority (outside of the UK's Judiciary), or even from some religious or principled action (such as the adoption of justice and humanity) that will usurp the current-day feminist influence in Family lawmaking. It could be something less dramatic: with Family Courts downgraded, or the courts tiring of feminists demanding decisions that are clearly wrong, or simply that feminism dies out, (along with its now quite-aged, hard-core matriarchs). What I do know is that the stripping of children from one parent, on the say-so of the other, is an outrageous abuse of both children and fathers and a great evil in our society that will not, forever, be tolerated.

A personal experience

In 2017, I was involved with the author Neil Lyndon in a new organisation called the Doubtfire Fund. Its stated aim was to raise money for a Class Action to get compensation for fathers who had been subjected to No Contact Orders with their children, where not supported by any Criminal or Public Law conviction.

Within six weeks of the Doubtfire Fund website going live, and Neil Lyndon's interview with the feminist Sir Mark Potter, a news item was run by the BBC, out of the blue and completely out of place with the stories of that time. The item, confusing even to the BBC news presenters on prime-time breakfast and evening news slots, was about how two unknown twin-boys had been brought up by their mother alone, after their father was given a No Contact Order by the Family Courts. The substance of the item was merely some shots of the now-adult boys saying how they thought it had been a good thing in their lives. There was no comment from the father, a few bitchy remarks from the mother, and no explanation of why this story was of any interest to the public.

Within maybe a month-and-a-half the *Victoria Derbyshire Show* aired, in three successive mornings, a low-quality piece, by a female freelance video producer, on fathers who had killed their children and why this necessitated more No Contact Orders to be made in the Family Courts. A key witness for this piece was a mother who had seemingly driven her husband to murder his children, two boys, by continually returning to the courts to try and gain a No Contact Order – something she failed to get. During one of her ex-husband's few allowed visits with his children, he had tragically taken them into the attic after setting his house on fire, killing himself and his children. A representative from FNF England was part of a panel of nearly all women, when Victoria Derbyshire, after calling James Hunt a c*nt, asked him a question in which she said they had, "… followed the trail of dead babies to fathers who should have had No Contact Orders."

In all of these programmes, if the word 'Jews' or 'blacks' was said instead of 'fathers', the presenter and producer would now be in prison for inciting racial hatred. Yet, given our times, all were allowed to speak as though men are a lower species.

I was one of many who wrote in to complain about the programme, (and had their complaint brushed aside), pointing out that just as many mothers as fathers are driven to annihilate themselves and their children. That these were complex incidents that happen for very different reasons, and affected a small number of people, but are gender-neutral in their occurrence.

Shortly after this feminist-led article by the BBC a Civil Service department, within the Department of Justice, announced the drafting of changes to Family Law to make the reversal of No Contact Orders harder to achieve, and their use more widespread. I have no idea whether these proposals did come through in Practice Directions or Law Acts, (maybe they are still on the way), but the mechanisms of feminist influence were for me, in this experience, clearly exposed.

Works cited, but not referenced in the text

14. *BBC Equality Information Report*. [2015/16].
15. **Collins, William**. [(Online) www.empathygap.uk (2019)]. See also *Further Reading* appendix in this book.
16. **Hicks, Joe; Allen, Grahame**. *A Century of Change*. [House of Commons Research Paper No. 99/11 (21st December, 1999)].
17. **Jaye, Cassie**. *The Red Pill* – video rushes from. [Interview with Erin Pizzey, published on YouTube (2016)].
18. *Lone parents with dependent children by marital status of parent, sex, UK 1996–2015*. [ONS April, 2016, Ref: 005660].
19. *Lone Parent and Step families with dependent children and children eligible for child maintenance*. [ONS March 2016, Ref: 005452].
20. Institute for Government website report on gender balance in the Civil Service. (1991–2019).

10

Redressing the Imbalance in Legal Aid

Since new restrictions on Legal Aid for Private Law Family Court cases came into force, State funding of Family Court cases has become viewed, by some, as one of the main mechanisms of discrimination against fathers. It is nowadays seen as a mother-only perk – especially for low-income families or those on benefits. While I fully respect the strength of feeling on this point, most fathers facing an ex fully tooled-up by the State still have opportunities to leverage Legal Aid in one way or another.

WHEN A FATHER DOES GET LEGAL AID

There are circumstances where a father may get Legal Aid, which can include:

a) Where social services are involved with a family and are considering taking the child from both parents.
b) Where a Family Court case has been allocated to the High Court.
c) Where there is a risk of child abduction out of the country by the mother.
d) If the mother is claiming violent domestic abuse by the father, it may be possible to get the State to fund a barrister to question her, to protect the mother from further abuse in the court.
e) Where a father is the resident parent, which normally means the mother has been put in custody, abandoned her children, or is mentally or physically incapacitated, and the father can prove a claim of domestic abuse by her.
f) Where the child has a guardian appointed by the court as a result of both parties claiming abuse of the child by the other, and where this protection is in place, it is possible that all parties will receive Legal Aid.

BENEFITING FROM THE EX'S LEGAL AID

Even though a father may not have a State-funded legal team, and his ex has, a father can still benefit in certain circumstances, (which are likely to change, so you need to check each of these with the agency):

1) At the time of writing, if your ex has Legal Aid for a MIAM meeting, then you can claim it for free as well.
2) If your ex has a Legal Aid for the main court case and you do not have a solicitor in your legal team, then the other side pays for the production of all court bundles. This rule might seem unimportant but bundle production is a major undertaking and takes up a lot of time for LiPs. If done correctly, so that your documents do not get left out and you get a bundle before the day of the hearing, it can be a major saving.
3) If there is an expert witness to be appointed in a court case, where both sides are equally represented, the person wanting the expert will pick up the whole tab. Often,

it is the father who wants such expert reports as he tries to overcome a report from CAFCASS. However, if the other side has Legal Aid then they can be ordered to pay half the cost even if the report is not one they want.

4) In civil litigation, the losing side may well be ordered to pay for the other side's legal team in its entirety. This sort of order is an 'order for costs'. While it is not usual in Child Arrangements Dispute cases, it is something pushed for when both parties have solicitors and one side is seen as having made an unrealistic application. However, if the other side is funded by Legal Aid, costs are unlikely to be asked for as if the unfunded side had won their case they would not have been allowed to ask for costs from a Legal Aid funded person.

Finally, if the Legal Aid funded side is asking for extra things like a Fact-Finding, more expert reports, a Section 7 CAFCASS report, and the unfunded party is arguing they are not necessary, they can point out that, (in addition to objections to the need for such reports), the other side is Legal Aid financed and that the court therefore has a special duty to ensure the expenditure of time and money is really necessary for justice. This argument is not a strong one, but it may help tip the balance of judgment.

REMOVING LEGAL AID FROM THE OTHER PARTY

I have seen people who have had their Legal Aid removed trying to pick up their case from their lawyers and I can tell you the courts are merciless with them. It can be an effective weapon in the war of the courtroom, especially if you make sure you have a barrister in all subsequent hearings. Losing representation, even at the very last minute, is no reason in the eyes of a court for delaying or extending any part of the court process.

Never bring up the issue of false or out-of-date information used by the other side to get Legal Aid with either the Judge in a case or the other side's solicitor. The only people you need to discuss this with are the Legal Aid Agency, who will allow appeals against Legal Aid certificates (awards of funding) in a defined process. You need to check with their advice line on how this works at the time of your case. If you find yourself curtly rebuffed (and remember the agency is very sensitive to people falsely trying to remove aid from ex-partners), there is always the option of sending in a letter with your information – something the Civil Service has to consider if sent as a complaint.

It can be a bit cat-and-mouse with the Legal Aid Agency who on the one hand have to protect the other party's data, and on the other hand have a duty to recover funds where fraudulently claimed. Still, you should be able to guess if not from your long relationship, then from the responses given in the C1A and other forms, or even from what is written in a witness statement, what information has been used by your ex to get Legal Aid. Often exaggerations are about ongoing criminal proceedings, which typically are manufactured for the express purpose of getting funding, and frequently the CPS has not yet decided to charge anyone for what is claimed in a Legal Aid application. If there are no falsehoods around the documents used to prove domestic abuse, then the next most frequent fraud is about means. Remember capital gains in a house counts towards the savings limit, (at least at the time of going to press), and that limit is very low. Declaring all income and all benefits is also something people tend to lie about to the Legal Aid Agency.

Finally, if you survive a Fact-Finding Hearing, where allegations of abuse are not proven against you, (regardless of the integrity of documents used in the other party's funding application), this can automatically remove the opposing side's Legal Aid. In this last situation you should immediately contact the agency and give them a copy of the hearing's judgment as soon as that hearing is over.

TWO CAN PLAY THAT GAME

FNF-BPM Wales (Families Need Fathers – Both Parents Matter) has come to specialise in helping fathers get legal aid by using legislation normally employed by women claiming domestic abuse against their ex, (as in theory this is meant to be gender-neutral). FNF-BPM's service stems from a particularly strong need in Wales where many men estranged from their children are economically worse-off than their brother-fathers elsewhere. FNF-BPM claims to have succeeded in getting legal representation for hundreds of fathers, based on their CDA (Claims of Domestic Abuse) against the mother of their children.

FNF-BPM Wales has published a three-step roadmap for fathers wanting to get Legal Aid:

1.   Check if you financially qualify for Legal Aid

Legal Aid is governed by a complex set of rules, regulations and bureaucratic processes that are continually shifting. The first advice is, therefore, to do a quick check if you might be eligible using one of those annoying online tools which can be found on the Gov.uk website. **(The exact address is given in Appendix IV)**. Legal Aid for a court case is different from Legal Aid for a MIAM meeting and different from Legal Help – which does not pay for litigation.

If you are too wealthy, or have too many savings, it is possible to get Legal Aid with a contribution from yourself. However, if your means are far higher than the Legal Aid criteria, you are left with the above options for leveraging the other party's aid.

2.   Check the merits of your case

As a father, this is a problem as this can only be done with a solicitor. Yet, any solicitor is likely to rule you out straight away because you are a man (and over 75 per cent of Family Law solicitors with Legal Aid are women). Objections are usually based on an assessment that your case lacks merit — without even considering it — and that you do not fit a Legal Aid requirement – without specifying this criterion.

When a solicitor says that your case has no merits, he or she (normally she) will not submit the necessary paperwork for you to the Legal Aid Agency. You may then be told that you can apply on your own, without a solicitor, (something I strongly advise against). However, even if a solicitor does agree your case has merit, it does not automatically mean you will pass the merits test as an adjudicator in the Legal Aid Agency has to also agree.

If you are sure your case does have merits, meaning a good chance of winning, when your solicitor has said it doesn't, as a father it is worth persevering. A good ploy is to pay for a barrister to give a written opinion and then take this back to your original solicitor, (if the barrister's opinion is positive). If the original solicitor then refuses to see you again, or still denies your case has merit, then try another one who is registered for Legal Aid – there are plenty to choose from.

If you fail at this step, do not despair. It is worth revisiting your Legal Aid entitlement as your court case progresses. Things may arise (for example CAFCASS may voice concerns over the neglect of your children by their mother) that suddenly open the doors to funding. This advice particularly applies if you are involved in an appeal case and you pass, without Legal Aid, the written or verbal permission stage of your application.

3. Get domestic violence evidence

In the past, this was the hardest part of the process, but FNF-BPM seems to have found a method, which may work for you or may only work in a particular region. FNF-BPM's approach relies on the LASPO 2012 Act Schedule 1 paragraphs 12 and 17, as well as the document: *Legal Aid, Sentencing and Punishment of Offenders Act (LASPO) 2012 – Evidence Requirements for Private Family Law Matters*. This latter document details what the Legal Aid Agency needs to satisfy the LASPO 2012 Act, which in paragraph 12 is:

"… an appropriate health professional referral to a domestic violence support service."

In paragraph 17, this same document stipulates you need a:

"… letter from an organisation providing domestic violence support services."

FNF-BPM has devised templates for a letter a doctor can use to refer a father to a domestic-violence support organisation, as well as forms for assessment of domestic-abuse victims. The referral letter can be found on FNF-BPM's website (**which I reference in Appendix IV**). In addition, the charity provides help via a service called AEGIS. This is a specialist, domestic-violence support service for fathers who have suffered, or are at risk of suffering, domestic abuse (in all its looney-tune, multi-various definitions, e.g. emotional, economic, verbal, and so on).

FNF-BPM has ironed-out obstacles that have in the past been thrown up against fathers attaining Legal Aid in this way. For example, the FNF-BPM referral form must be signed by the father at the bottom, to confirm consent for the sharing of his details with others **only** to provide help and support. Otherwise, it may be rejected on the grounds that FNF-BPM does not meet all data protection criteria. Also, a GP or nurse must not only put their name on the letter of referral, they must give their registration number as well, and then sign and use their practice stamp to confirm their details.

If a referral from a medical practitioner is in writing, then this should be sent to FNF-BPM, at legalaid@fnf-bpm.org.uk, or by post to: Legal Aid Department, FNF BPM Cymru, 61 Cowbridge Road East, Cardiff, CF11 9AE. For anything to be effective with the Legal Aid Agency this referral must meet the LASPO 2012, paragraph 12 criteria. FNF-BPM can confirm receipt of a referral as another way of fulfilling this requirement. The AEGIS service can then assess a father to see if he is a victim of domestic abuse, and provide the paperwork needed to prove this assessment. All of this documentation could give the requisite evidence the Legal Aid Agency requires for an applicant to be funded as a domestic violence/abuse victim, as detailed in the LASPO 2012 Act and Agency Rules.

Importantly, as a consequence of the madness of feminist-inspired Family Law legislation, a father does not need to have experienced domestic violence, nor does his doctor need to confirm he has suffered domestic violence, for this method to work. A doctor only needs to confirm that a father may be at risk of such violence and that he has been given a referral to a support organisation as a result.

A word of warning: while a full and free legal team is a considerable force to go up against as a LiP, when you get one you will find that because of how much they are paid, and because of Family Court biases, the service you get as a father is typically diabolical. What is more, this aid is given in lumps, with a pause between each, which can be very disruptive to the smooth running of your case. At any of these stages when funding is reassessed a recipient of Legal Aid faces suddenly losing his legal team, for example, if his case has taken a turn for the worse.

An independently-paid-for legal team, of any constitution (see chapter six), will always give you the best chance of protecting your children through the Family Courts.

ALTERNATIVES TO LEGAL AID

At some point you will be told there are ways, other than Legal Aid, to get free legal representation. Pro Bono units are often mentioned. These are where a newly qualified barrister can gain experience by providing free barrister services. Forget this! The Pro Bono service is sparse, only deals with simple cases, and is unreliable.

Similarly, there is a free service for LiPs in some courts called the Personal Support Unit (PSU) – **see Appendix IV for details**. This service consists of well-meaning people who will help you file papers at the Court Office, show you where your courtroom is, and make encouraging noises. They may be useful if you are truly on your own, at least in helping you carry your bundles.

McKenzie Friends are often approached for free help, but in reality few will do this for no money and if they do, it will only be for part of your case. A lot of people will seem willing to help in support groups, but usually this free enthusiasm dries up as a case drags on.

In the end, there is no substitute for a free legal team, although you should bear in mind Legal Aid is meant to be a loan, recoverable when your finances improve – although I have rarely seen this happen except where the case itself yields money or assets to someone it financed.

11

McKenzie Friend Advice – Case Strategy

"An emerging consensus is that... a minimum of one-third of time is necessary to achieve the benefits [of two involved parents] and that these benefits continue to accrue as parenting time reaches equal (50-50) time." Fabricius, W.V.; Braver, S.L.; Diaz, P. & Velez, C.E. (2010) *Custody and parenting time: Links to family relationships and wellbeing after divorce.* In **Lamb, M.** (Ed) *The father's role in child development.* [(5th Ed), pp201-260. Wiley & Sons: New Jersey].

PLAYING THE LEGAL GAME

Here I address how to construct the core argument for a Family Law CAP court case. As always, I endeavour to stick to legal terminology but in this chapter my language may be looser than elsewhere.

Throughout this book I have emphasised the importance of forward planning, for example, in deciding a budget of time and money for your litigation. As to go to court without such preparation is like trying to build a house, in your spare time, with only a belief that as things come up you will find solutions by thinking hard about them.

In the same way, you should prepare the core of your argument for the child arrangements you want, to see how these fit within the constraints of the Family Court legal process. Consider this the ground survey of your project, after which you can apply to the authorities (the courts) to go ahead with what you want.

THE CONSTITUENT PARTS OF A COURT CASE

You should by now realise that your argument about why you should be allowed to bring up your children in the way you want, (but in a way your ex is determined to prevent you from doing), isn't presented to a court in one splurge, in any one document, or one speech. Instead, court processes force you to produce a series of documents that constrain and dictate what you are supposed to say in each. You are also given a set of opportunities to provide proofs — whether written, recorded or spoken — in support of your argument, an argument that has to be both legally feasible, supported by evidence, and appealing to a Judge's version of common sense.

By the time you get to a Final Hearing what you want to say may be sliced and diced in a series of items that may include (if you are the Applicant):

> Your Application form(s).
> A Position Statement.
> A Skeleton Argument document.
> A Chronology document.
> A Witness Statement(s).

Exhibits to your Witness Statement(s).
The respondent's Witness Statement(s).
Exhibits to the respondent's Witness Statement(s).
Expert Reports.
A summary narrative from a Judge in a Fact-Finding against some of the points in a Scott Schedule.
Your verbal clarification, made in the witness box, of your Witness Statement(s).
Comments made by you under cross-examination.
Comments made by you in re-cross.
A Section 7 report by CAFCASS.
A CAFCASS report following Schedule 2 letters.
Comments made in cross-examination by the respondent, against her Witness Statement(s).
Comments made by experts in support of their position and under cross-examination.
Comments made by CAFCASS in a Section 7 report in support of their position and under cross-examination.
Your submission at the end of the trial.
Your reading list, given to a Judge just before he considers the case.

The question is: how does a Judge make a decision out of all this crap? For that matter, how do you pull all this stuff together into a coherent argument? An argument which, if you were given 45 minutes to speak as freely as you want, with answering questions perhaps an-hour-and-a-half, you could clearly put across why a court should order what you want and why what the mother wants is not in the interests of your children.

The answer to the question 'how' is that although your case is scattered across all of the above items you should ensure arguments are **consistently repeated** in each, rather than relying on a reasoning that requires a mind to follow a knitting-together of pieces of a case. Consider each item a new test of your argument(s).

When you cannot directly control the content of a piece of evidence, for example, if a CAFCASS report sides with the mother's point of view, you need to add things that modify it, for example, by exploiting the time the social worker spends in the witness box. In this last case, you should use this time to bring out those things that a Cafcass worker does agree with, and discredit as misinformed or stubborn, those things with which she disagrees. For example, she may be led to disagree with absolutely everything you say, which, even to a biased Judge, will undermine her testimony. Tripping up Cafcass workers on the details of your children's lives, and the circumstances of the case, may also be part of this line of questioning, (or part of a written retort in your Witness Statement). Removing negative items on legal technicalities, or trumping them with contradicting things of higher value (in the eyes of the court), are equally valid ploys if opportunities present themselves.

In short, use whatever it takes to win, either in writing or in advocacy. Be tenacious in defence of arguments you have advanced, not nasty, but never concede a point even if it is seemingly lost (think: House of Commons question time). To do this, you need to be both attentive to criticism and clear about the ground upon which your case rests. To be clear necessitates that you know where you are going, which takes us to the starting point, which is where you want to end up.

START AT THE END

Once you are done with the courts, all you will have is a piece of paper, called a Court Order. The best place to start building your case is, therefore, writing down a version of the Final Order you want. Drafting an order may seem a simple thing to do, but first, you have to consider what orders a Family Court Judge can make. It is possible that what you want is not something a court can put in an order, or give in the way you want. **Refer to Appendix I** and the list of orders possible in a CAP Private Law Family Court case.

Order templates

Once you are sure of which types of orders you are looking to get, you can try and make use of what Judges use to write orders, i.e. templates.

At first you may write the order you want in freehand, saying anything. It is then worth trying to fill in a template with the legal words you hope a Judge will use. Going through this exercise can inform you of other aspects of the legal process which need to be considered at the start of your application, or other applications you need to make in addition to a Section 8 application, as well as what Interim Orders you might need before the Final Order. This investigation might even give you hints about how best to fill in an initial application form.

Sir James Munby issued a bunch of order templates for Private Family Law in March 2018, and published these on the Judiciary.gov.uk website. These were later removed. Order templates can still be found on the internet, but their location keeps changing (so you may have to hunt around a bit). There are now two options for Judge Order templates, with some saying the latter replaces the former. Judges can fill in pre-worded forms, which are known as CAP01-04 templates, or they can use their own words but tick off items from a list Sir Munby produced for each order type. Pre-worded order templates cover all eventualities, so you will need to delete those sections not wanted.

Some people may find both types of template too dry or complicated. If so, it may be an idea to instead get hold of a CAFCASS parenting plan template instead, and fill it in with how you would like your child arrangements made, and then try and go from that to the wording of an order.

If at all possible, once you have drafted the order(s) you want, try and get a legal expert to give an opinion on it, i.e. the chances of a Family Court granting it, given your circumstances. Failing this, consult a Father's Support Forum, or a McKenzie Friend – although the best person for this task would be a barrister. Such a discussion on the order you are after may force you to rewrite the order(s) into something more attainable, which should also mean your application to the court becomes more realistic as well.

Your backstop position

Discussion about your target order should also force you to consider your absolute backstop position. Think in terms of a situation where you have applied for a Family Court Order but you lose, and there is nothing you can do about it. What would be the absolute minimum you could accept? What, for instance, does it feel like to agree with what the mother wants (unless it's no contact at all, in which case never agree)? Reread chapter two and write this position down, however distasteful.

In the hurly-burly of a court case when you start getting decisions, reports or pieces of evidence that unexpectedly stack up against you a father can panic and give away too much, especially when he is presented with an on-the-spot way out of a court case that is seemingly going wrong. By the time a father realises what he's done he is often already out of the court building. There then can start a commonly seen cycle of repeated applications to the courts that progressively wears a man down. A pre-prepared backstop can be a vital aid in these situations, and it is something only you can do.

UNDERSTANDING THE CORE OF YOUR CASE FOR THE ORDER YOU WANT

To gain an order from a court, you need to present an argument to make it possible for a court to agree to it. Barristers call this their case theory, something you or I would call a 'core argument'. This argument can come from turning the order you want into a question(s). In nearly all cases for fathers this comes down to: **how do you argue that you should have more time with your children than a mother wants to give?** In your case, it may be this question, or something different, or this and something else. Writing the order you want, and then outlining the question you have to answer, may help clarify what you are trying to get out of the court, and in doing so greatly increase your ability to cope with the court process.

Your legal argument

Most people think they know how to argue their corner; it is something a lot of us have to do every day at work. Yet, a court is a different barrel of fish. Firstly, you are not dealing with a common-sense situation. Arguments in court can be handled under a process of legal argument, or by a common-sense process very different from that used 'down the pub'. There is little point, therefore, in testing out arguments you are going to use in court with a friend or relative. However, there is a lot to be gained from learning the basics of the 'legal argument' process.

A legal argument is about proving that your case fits the conditions in the law you want to rely on to allow or force a court to make the order you want, by setting up a 'legal test'. This test is a type of thought-exercise where you try and connect the sections of law you want to invoke with conditions that must be met.

Determining a legal test can become tricky, and very quickly you will see why a solicitor is sometimes a valuable member of a litigation team. Conditions for a test can in some instances be easily found, as they sit within the same section of the Law Act as the law you want to evoke. At other times they may be scattered somewhere else in the same Act, or not obviously anywhere, but requiring a detailed understanding of a number of Law Acts. As an example, in chapter seven I referred to PR being given automatically to a father even if he is not named on a birth certificate as long as he later marries the mother of his child. This legal argument is based on The Legitimacy Act 1976, which is only tangentially mentioned in the CA 1989 at the point it discusses PR.

The final step in a legal argument is to get the court to allow you to bring evidence into the case that is both reliable in the eyes of a court and satisfies your legal test. (NB: Any evidence in a court case requires the permission of the court to enter it). Information given in Witness Statements and verbal 'evidence in chief', (clarification in the witness box of Witness Statements), count as evidence, along with anything reliably written and lawfully included in the court bundle.

Where there is no direct evidence available, or possible, to prove a condition of law has been or will be met, the applicant can ask the court to make an assumption, or projection, from other evidence. This is especially so if the argument is that making the order you want will cause those conditions to be met.

Lastly, a person can invite a court to conclude it is reasonable to assume a legal test has been met, self-evidently, meaning without any evidence or projections. For example, if a law required a person to be the mother of a child, you could say that this has self-evidently been met without needing to have a maternity test or medical examination simply because no one in a case has disputed this fact. It is in a way just stating what everyone has already assumed, without being aware of this assumption.

If part of your case is a legal argument, you therefore need to build up pieces of evidence to support your argument by asking in preliminary hearings for these to be included in the Final Hearing bundle. These evidences need to show that the conditions for the law you want to use to get your preferred order have been met, or imply that they will be best met by the situation that would be created if the court made the order you want. For example, you may argue for evidences that show the arrangements you want for your child or children will best meet the Welfare Checklist, contained in the subsections of CA 1989 section 1 (3).

However, what makes this process really tricky is that a legal argument is not a static thing. It is something that evolves as evidence is brought into a court case by either side. Another task that therefore follows on from this is that a party to a court case (let's say the applicant) must also identify the legal test for the law under which the respondent's preferred order can be made, and show that based on evidence these tests have **not** been met, or not met as well as for the case of the applicant.

As well as things being thrown into this boiling cauldron of thought during the preliminary hearings, in the Final Hearing there is an interrogation of statements. This process tries to knock away items of evidence vital to a legal argument, through **what** is said in response to questions **and the way it is said**. However, if enough evidence survives then the plunger of a legal-pinball-machine fires a ball, the legal point, into the pinball machine, the Judge's head, and it bounces around scoring a random amount of points. The more legal arguments you can launch in this way the higher the score in the mind of the Judge and the more likely, in theory, you get the order you want. Or so the story goes.

As an example, imagine a case where the biological father applies for a child arrangement order and in reply the mother writes on her C7 form that the court should dismiss the father's application without a hearing as he, "Has no right to make it." She says: she kicked him out of the family home following a separation, and "From that time to this he hasn't seen his kids. They don't know him anymore and they have a new daddy. He hasn't been involved in their lives at all."

The father may present a spoken legal argument in defence at the FHDRA, that CA 1989 section 10 (4)a gives the court powers to make a Section 8 order (the Law Act that will allow the father's application to be heard), on the application of **any** parent of a child, (the legal test), and the father then states, (the evidence), that he is the father of the children named in his application.

Let us say that in this example the mother, during the FHDRA, then disputes that the applicant is the father, but does not say why. Then the father offers the court copies of birth certificates as new evidence, naming him as the father of the children in question. Although the court has not authorised introduction of this evidence, rules of evidence and disclosure in the Family Courts are very loose and so the court allows this inclusion. A copy of the certificate is then handed to the Judge, and another copy to the mother for comment, and this is then added to the fledgling court bundle.

This process could go on and on. For if the mother was so minded she could look at Section 10 (9) CA 1989, for example, where there is a clause about a court having to be mindful of the connection of a parent with a child before allowing an application. However, let us say she is unaware of this argument, but that the court, who is aware of this argument, also notes the father has stated he has maintained contact with his children, (and so expects this to be included in this statement he has yet to be ordered to be produced). So the court schedules another hearing with Witness Statements to be given on this issue, with the intention of having a Fact-Finding on the matter if the issue of disputed involvement is repeated in those statements, or if the CAFCASS report is unclear on this point.

In short, a legal argument is about finding a section of some legal rule or Law Act that compels the court to give you something you want, or allows the court to order something you want. The engine is the legal test, and the fuel is evidence. A legal argument is not static as it is both a proposition to the court, and defence to counterarguments from the other party. During a court case, counterarguments will emerge in interim hearings as disclosures are made, or new evidence is included, and these change the nature of your argument by default. Most importantly, it is best practice to have your legal argument thought-out before you even apply to the courts.

Mandatory legal tests

There are certain legal tests, or legal arguments, which have to be met in any application by a father for fair apportionment of time with his children, and before a court can give any order:

1. That the applicant has a legal right to make the application regarding the named child – see Section 10 & 91 (14) of CA 1989.
2. That the father has met pre-application requirements, e.g. MIAMs – see Family Court Practice Direction (FPD) 12B para 8 (1-4).
3. The application is not so bad that it can be struck out – see FPD 4A.
4. That there is no current risk of harm to the children from either parent – see FPD 12B para 13.
5. That the applicant has taken all reasonable steps to find an out-of-court settlement with the respondent – see FPD 12B paras 6.3 & 14.3 (mediation).
6. That the child or children would benefit from an order rather than things being left as they are at the time of the application – see Section 1 (5) CA 1989.
7. That the order applied for meets the Welfare Checklist for the children – see Section 1 (3) CA 1989.

Initial forms, such as C100, in an application deal with points 1-3. The initial CAFCASS safety report or letter to be delivered at an FHDRA Hearing deals with point 4. The remaining points (5–7) **must be** added by you, usually in your Witness Statement, as what I call 'boilerplate points'.

The pecking order of evidence

Clearly, any argument, a legal or common sense one, depends on proof to some degree or other. In a Family Court Child Arrangements dispute there is a special problem as both parties know everything there is to know about each other's lives. As a consequence, the same events and actions are present to a court to mean totally different things and support opposing arguments. For a Judge, there are a few ways out of this dilemma. One is to hold an official Fact-Finding Hearing, if the disputed facts venture into allegations of abuse. Another is simply to decide out of personal preference, or follow the preference of a social worker involved in the case – **and both methods are legal**. However, there is also a self-evident pecking order of evidence in a hearing, a bit like the card game Trumps, or Whist. This is not written down anywhere, nor is it agreed, but it is an observation of those who have spent a lot of time in law courts.

A sworn statement, that something is so, is evidence. This in turn is beaten by a sworn statement by someone who also makes themselves available for questioning in a Final Hearing. However, this is normally trumped by a statement with something else (if directly related), such as a certificate, letter or something that can be shown to the court as an attachment to the Witness Statement.

There are a whole raft of things you can attach to Witness Statements, some of which you would think should not count, but do. Printed copies of emails always make me mad as these are so easily forgeable, with Photoshop, as are any printouts of social media postings. It is also entirely feasible to fake emails, by hacking an account of someone you know well and sending an email from them to you; one that is, for example, abusive. I'm afraid that, nonetheless, such copies of emails, social media comments, texts, and even handwritten accounts of telephone conversations, are usually readily accepted and a lot of weight is often put on them in court unless someone can prove they are fakes.

A Witness Statement backed by such attachments, for example a letter or copy of an email, is then trumped by a statement backed by an expert report, if that report is specifically about that statement and not a general commentary on an issue raised in a statement. A CAFCASS report is one of the highest cards to play in the evidence game, if it agrees with your argument, but this can be trumped by an expert report – if you can get a court to agree to have one included. NB: There are strict rules of procedure for the inclusion of an expert report, such as from a Child Psychologist (see chapter four), because of the weight placed on this evidence.

Known as the 'Rule of 12', a statement from a child over the age of 12 years old is pretty much on a par with a CAFCASS report, whereas statements from children below this age may not weigh at all. Finally, the slam-dunk trump-card in any court case is any fact found in a Fact-Finding Hearing.

Past Appeal Court cases, or scientific findings on a subject, that help an argument are not, in my opinion, evidence so much as assistance to a court on a principle not defined in Law Acts.

A final consideration is the murky factor of relevance. Even though a piece of evidence may be backed up with the best possible authority it is no good if it does not self-evidently prove a point. For example, an email sent from one party to the other that says something like:

"You will never see your kids again," is self-evidently proof of abuse or intimidation. Whereas an email that says: "I'm coming to get the kids at 2pm," could be intimidation if the normal time for pick-up was 5pm. However, this latter communication can also be explained any number of different ways, whereas the former email is difficult to justify except as a threat. A great deal of so-called 'evidence' in Family Court cases tends to fall into this latter category, where people ask a court to accept their spin on documents, that without a convoluted explanation, do not prove anything at all.

In summary, my advice to a Family Court litigant-father is to take stock of the evidence they have in-hand before applying to a court. Not only its content, but **what weight a court will put on it**. A father should then use this audit to temper an application in terms of what to expect. It is also important to remember, when making this appraisal, that Criminal and Civil Law are separate branches of the law. Each takes its own route through the courts, sometimes with very different conclusions over exactly the same evidence. Crime reports, while very useful for evoking PD 12J and for getting Legal Aid for mothers, do little for fathers.

In nearly all the applications to the Family Courts I have seen a father's initial cache of evidence to support his arguments mostly consists of hopes, i.e. for what will be uncovered if a Judge makes the Directions he wants. This weakness is not often appreciated by fathers whose aspirations for orders, while totally reasonable in the world of common sense, are overly demanding of the Family Court process.

Top Tip: Family Courts tend to arrive at judgments using CAFCASS reports and a Judge's personal preference (the 'Judge Judy' approach). If a father's court case relies on the use of other evidence, as is often the situation, he must **entice** a court to use it. To do this his proof has to be both self-evidently relevant (i.e. not requiring any verbal explanation), and highly trustworthy (i.e. a high-card in the evidence game). It is a massive mistake for a father to fill a court bundle with documents of tangential importance, even if that is what the other party has done.

Catch-22 of legal arguments for a father

A legal argument can be a robust way of compelling a court to give an order you want, and is far better than relying on common sense. However, for fathers the processes of legal argument — of defining an order, the law that supports the giving of that order, arguing a test that determines the applicability of that law and then providing evidence that this legal test has been met — all very quickly falls off a cliff.

Once you have proven that: you are entitled to make an application for a Child Arrangements Order, that you have exhausted all reasonable out-of-court options for resolving the dispute, that your case is also not an unworthy one, that a 'no order' is not better in your case than an order, and that your proposed order satisfies the Welfare Checklist, you then face a legislative black-hole. For there is **no legislation of any sort** about the core thing the 51,000 couples a year who walk into Family Courts want to be settled, namely: how much time a child should spend with each of its separated parents.

Daft, isn't it?

You cannot prove, for example, that you meet the requirements of a law that allows or compels a court to order a child to spend 10, 20, 30 or 50 per cent of their time outside of school with you, as there are no laws on this point and therefore no legal arguments to use. You can prove that it is in the best interests of a child in your case to have contact with you, but in law, thanks to Hale's CA 1989, this can be a letter once a year.

It is not the same for mothers.

Alleging abuse takes a court case out of the realm of evidence. From the outset, a Family Court is **obliged** to behave in a certain way and accept the allegations as real until you as a father can prove yourself innocent. If a mother wants you to have limited contact, or no contact with your children, this is a neat trick as the legal test for a court to accept allegations is basically: are there any allegations?

It is impossible to protect against an allegation of domestic abuse. Getting some sort of CRB certificate clearing you, before or now, is not possible (if only)! Once domestic abuse allegations enter a court case you have started you simply have to accept that the process is now made up of two connected court cases: a defence of claims of domestic abuse, and an application for shared, or sole, residency of your children.

Other ways of putting an argument

After hitting the buffers of 'legal argument' a lot of fathers then attempt to draw on other documents, such as Case Law, to tease out the reasons why the Welfare Checklist is best met by shared-parenting of their children.

It is true that the use of non-legal sources is allowable where things are unclear in law. However, documents need to be very authoritative, such as the publication by the erstwhile HMSO, *Children Act 1989 Guidance and Regulations*.

However, there is a problem with both these documents and Case Law. Firstly, the Civil Service has got wise to an educated populous that uses the internet and can copy, slice, dice and distribute anything printed in a matter of moments. As a result, they have 'gone dark'. HMSO is no longer. In fact, the reason for Neil Lyndon's interview with the President of the Family Division, quoted in chapter two, was because he was sure there was some guidance or directive document that explained the clear and obvious pattern of behaviour of the Family Courts against fathers.

Secondly, as far as Case Law is concerned, the main issue is that these come from Higher Court Cases, after the Lower Courts have already dealt with them, usually in an appeal. This means they do not deal with evidence. Yet, the apportionment of time with a child is very much a matter of evidence.

You can look, but I have never seen anything that gives legal precedent as to how much time should be given to a father and under what conditions. Especially, I have never seen apportionment of time with a child between two separated parents related to how well they meet the Welfare Checklist, in any High Court judgment.

Fathers often ask about arguing on principle, using statistics or the science of psychology, to show in some way a father must have a certain amount of time with their children, or otherwise harm will be caused (as, for example, shown in the quote at the start of this chapter). However, again we have a problem.

There is no doubt at all that there is a systematic methodology for handling apportionment of time between separated parents that is common across all Family Courts. This method is transparent from the identical orders that are made under the same conditions. So what a father is asking in arguing for a decision based on a principle, that has not to-date been applied, is for a change to a court methodology. This effectively is asking a Lower Court to make a High Court decision, or have a mini-Judicial Review and then immediately apply the conclusion or new principle to a case. Yes, you can try. Yet, in my opinion, it simply cannot be done.

So the question still remains: as a father how do you argue for a fair proportion of time with your children?

All that a father has left is common sense. Yet, again, we have a problem. Firstly, a normal person shapes common-sense arguments around the feedback from a listener, using the way they respond to what is said. However, while Judges in courts can give feedback it is minimal, and this greatly undermines anyone's ability to argue on this basis.

Secondly, what we call common sense is not what a Judge would call sense within a Family Court Hearing. For example, Judges use a precept that compels them, once other conditions are met, to give fathers no more contact with their children than every other weekend and half the holidays. Where is this rule written down? Just like most of the mechanisms of misandry in the Family Courts it isn't written down anywhere. Using common sense therefore means, unlike with legal arguments, you have to construct propositions without being allowed to see the relevant rulebook. All you can do is guess what the hidden rules say, even if this means shooting in the dark – see the next chapter.

12

McKenzie Friend Advice –
Before Applying to the Courts

Once you have some idea about what order you want, who it is that is going to be on your litigation team, how much money and time you have to do this project, and how you hope to get evidence for the order you want, it is then time to draft some paperwork **before** filling in a C100 application form.

The core documents I would pre-prepare are:

☞   A draft of the order you want (see the last chapter).

☞   A Chronology of your life-events leading up to your separation and dispute over child arrangements.

☞   A draft Witness Statement.

WHY WRITE A DRAFT WITNESS STATEMENT?

Firstly, the C100 form often bears the brunt of an angry father desperate to argue a case and get things going. Writing a draft Witness Statement before filling in a C100 form ensures that the application is coherent and not stuffed with things that should go elsewhere. Secondly, the process of pre-writing a Witness Statement can help you see where you need more evidence. Thirdly, as the court sausage-machine grinds through your litigation it requires different information to do its stuff at different stages, and this means you have to repeat yourself. In this repetition, you cannot afford to make errors of consistency as in the final, deciding, hearing any mistakes, however innocent, will be seized upon as indications of falsehoods. Finally, drafting a Witness Statement along with an order and chronology, at the beginning of your case, gives you a head start when responding to the other party's documents – which can land on your kitchen table a couple of days before a hearing.

There is no right or wrong method for writing a statement. Many people prefer to write down what I call a 'chain of consciousness' – putting everything that is in their heads in whatever sequences it comes to them. However, a chain of consciousness statement is difficult to match and amend to a respondent's counter-statement or other evidence such as a CAFCASS or an expert report, which is why after letting-off steam, you should try and translate your statement into a good first draft.

FROM THEORY TO PRACTICE – A FIRST DRAFT OF A WITNESS STATEMENT

I know a lot of this is redundant work; you will probably have to redo this first draft as things are included in the court case – although there is no limit on how many Witness Statements you can submit, with the permission of the court. Yet, this method of drafting a statement before writing an application helps in so many ways.

Writing style

Whichever way you draft your Witness Statement guard against letting your dislike of your ex come through in the way you write, and make sure the content of the statement is about what is best for your children, and not about what you want. Further, you should try and avoid the words 'contact', or 'contact parent', as well as 'resident parent', 'contact time', or 'overnight visits'. What you should talk about is the percentage of out-of-school time your children need to live with you, and in which of their two homes, together with a proposed schedule and why this meets the CA 1989 Family Law child(ren) Welfare Checklist better than their mother's proposals.

I recommend using a writing strategy that has both a contract and newspaper methodology. This strategy means making sure boilerplate phrases are covered off, while putting your whole case in the first one or two paragraphs, in short form, and then repeating your argument in the rest of the document, but in a lot more detail.

Sometimes people like to just go at the main argument and then top and tail this with legally necessary phrases. Others like to frame what they are about to say by starting with boilerplate and mandatory sentences, to get their writing-motor running, and then see what is left. You may even find it easier to run two documents: a common-sense argument, and a legal argument with key phrases, and then combine the two.

I have chosen to start this chapter with the statutory stuff, and then move on to a discussion of key common-sense propositions for shared-residence.

Legal rules (in Practice Directions) dictate the layout and what must be included in a Witness Statement as this is an official document. It can, for instance, be no more than 25 pages long, using A4 paper and 1.5 lines separation as a minimum. **See Appendix III** for an example of the layout of the front cover sheet of this document, which is similar to all other court bundle document headers. There is a link to the rules for preparing a court bundle **in Appendix IV.**

Boilerplate phrases and information

There is now a new form called: *Form C120: Witness Statement Template – Child arrangements – Parental Dispute.* This online form is an optional way of submitting a Witness Statement (**see Appendix IV for this link**). If you prefer making a traditional written statement, it may be worth using the headings from this downloadable form as discussion points. **See Figure 3.**

I believe a freehand Witness Statement gives you more latitude to say what you want rather than being restricted to lists of things on a form.

A traditional statement should start with something like this, (NB bold type is not needed):

I, Fred Bloggs, of, 22 The Street, Croydon, London, CR12 RY, will say as follows:

All the subsequent paragraphs must be numbered from this sentence onwards, and each page needs to have a number at the bottom. Each paragraph should be no more than 10 lines long. The first numbered paragraph of a Witness Statement should explain who you are and why you are making this application.

1. Do any of the children have any medical problems?
2. Did you and the other parent (or other party) live together?
3. Give brief details of the circumstances of your separation.
4. Describe the childcare arrangements in place between you and the other parent or party before the proceedings were issued?
5. When and how often did the other parent or party spend time with the child(ren)?
6. Give a brief description of the child(ren)'s routine during the week and at weekends. Advise how each parent or other party has been involved with such routines. Also give details of other family members who help or are available to help.
7. If you are in work, what are your working hours? If a child lives with you, who looks after the child when you are at work?
8. Describe the homes in which the child lives, stays or spends time. State whether it is a flat, maisonette or a house; with size (i.e. how many bedrooms?) and the sleeping arrangements for the child(ren) if they currently stay?
9. How far away do you live from the other parent or party?
10. How long does the journey take by public transport or car?
11. How far away is the child(ren)'s school from your home and describe how the child(ren) get to and from school.
12. Describe the child(ren)'s out-of-school activities, their hobbies and pastimes.
13. Describe each child's personality, likes and dislikes and any particular needs they may have.
14. Are there any concerns or issues about the child(ren)'s schooling?
15. Give your view as to the quality of the child(ren)'s past and current relationship with the other parent or party. Do you think that this needs to be improved, and if so, how can the court help you as parents to do that?
16. Describe how the child(ren) are coping with the separation of their parents and the current issues between you and the other parent or party.
17. What childcare and parenting arrangements are you asking the court to implement?
    Who do you say the child/children should live with? How much time should the child/children spend with the other parent or party or anyone else? Give your reasons for the arrangements you want.
18. Do you have any worries about the other parent's parenting abilities?
19. Have you or the children ever been involved with social services or the police?
20. What steps have you taken to reach an agreement with the other parent (or party) about the arrangements for the children? What is preventing you from being able to reach an agreement with the other parent (or party) in respect of the arrangements for the children?
21. What do you feel you can do to help the court in making a parenting order that will satisfy both parents and the children's welfare?
22. Give the court details of any other information that you consider relevant to the case.

Figure 3. Headings for Form C120.

For example:

1. *I am the father of Maximillian Bloggs-Waterstone, (DOB 04.05.08) with whom I have regular contact. I am named as the father on Max's birth certificate. Max lives with his mother, the respondent, Eileen Waterstone. I am making this statement in support of my application for a Child Arrangements Order in which Max would live with both his mother and me, on alternate weeks, starting on Sunday nights.*

Your statement should be written in the first person, as in 'I think', and throughout it should sound fair and reasonable.

If there is more than one order being applied for, separate your statement under headings that describe each type of order, e.g.

- *Shared-residency.*
- *Activity Directions to help stop parent-alienation of the child.*

Things that must be included

A court usually looks for a party's answers to the mandatory legal tests set out in chapter 11. The issues that are not covered by a CAFCASS report or your answers on the standard C100 application form are:

☑ That the applicant has taken all reasonable steps to find an out-of-court settlement with the respondent. FPD 12B para 6.3 & 14.3 (mediation).

☑ That the child or children would benefit from an order rather than things being left as they are at the time of the application – see section 1 (5) CA 1989.

☑ That the order applied for meets the Welfare Checklist for the children – see section 1 (3) CA 1989.

Your statement should be clear when making responses to these pieces of law, so that a Judge cannot infer an unintended response from something you have written elsewhere. One way to ensure your meaning is not misinterpreted is to draft your comments under a series of headings. You can decide later whether to amalgamate these remarks into the general text of your statement, or leave them as a list. For example, the Welfare Checklist is a series of items detailed in Section 1 (3) of the CA 1989. If left as a list, your responses might look like the following:

> *5. The ascertainable wishes and feelings of the child concerned (considered in the light of his age and understanding).*
> *My child (name) who is x years old, has made it clear he wants to live with his mother and me and is happy to have two homes. He has made this clear in a letter to the court, exhibit XY attached to this statement, as well as to the psychologist at paragraph 19.1 of his expert report dated dd/mm/yy.*
> *6. His physical, emotional and educational needs.*
> *There are no specific educational needs relevant to this application as both the respondent mother and I now live near my child's school. However, my son is a keen footballer and I am a retired footballer. My son has daily practice and previously benefited from my advice and emotional support on a*

daily basis. Should my son only see me at alternate weekends he would be very disappointed and his performance in his game would suffer. The respondent mother does not like or support football. A report, exhibit YX, from my son's coach indicates a deterioration in his football performance since the current arrangements started that exclude me from my son's life during the working week.

7. Likely effect on him of any change in his circumstances.

My son (name) has lived with me from birth, until my separation from the respondent six months ago. He loves both his parents and on those occasions he has been allowed to stay with me he has been comfortable in my new home. Both my son's mother and I have shared, equally, the role of primary carer throughout my son's life. This has meant that on some days I would see him to school and be there when he returns, and sometimes it was the respondent. The current situation of having only one home-parent during the week is a change of circumstances. My son would become depressed and lost, as indicated in the expert psychologist's report at para 18.2, should the current situation not be returned to the norm, through a shared residency order, at the earliest opportunity.

Attachments to a statement

Exhibits, or attachments, to a Witness Statement should have a front cover sheet and must be numbered; such as ML01, (where ML is the initials of the person giving the statement), followed by a name that indicates what the attachment is i.e. ML01 Letter from GP.

Exhibits to Witness Statements need to be referenced in the statement i.e. you can't attach something that is not part of what you say, as these belong in a separate section of the court bundle.

AVOIDING UNACCEPTABLE PROPOSITIONS

Given all that has previously been written in this book it should be apparent how important it is to exclude reasoning that will trip you up. In previous chapters I listed some of the prejudices courts use to undermine the common sense most of us reach for in arguing for shared-parenting (see chapter on Misandry in Family Law and Court Practices). However, most of these arguments are also central to any father's case – which is why the courts exclude them!

What you need to do is peel off the skin of the reasoning behind the axioms of bias so you can use what you need without being declared offside. What I present here are my best guesses of how prejudicial reasoning could sit in the minds of the opposition. I also make some suggestions about strategies for overcoming each prejudice.

However, every person's case is special and what works in one instance doesn't necessarily work in another, so don't rely on these propositions.

Shared-parenting is unworkable and harmful to children.

The reasoning is that there simply is not enough money after a divorce for both parents to run a full-size family home, (and property settlements from divorces and CSA maintenance claims see to this). More importantly, having two homes is unsettling at best, and probably harmful to a child's wellbeing, as children cannot cope with the disruption of moving every week or so (despite it being commonplace in America). Finally, this point connects to the idea that the abuse of a mother is abuse of a child. For a mother may be distressed if her children 'live' with rather than just visit a man she hates, (possibly to be mothered by a stepmother interloper). This distress is abuse of a child because it makes a mother unable to properly parent that child because she is distressed.

Science shows that the key amount of time a child should have with separated parents is a minimum of 33 per cent, (see the reference at the beginning of this chapter). This minimum is well above the average 7 per cent of time fathers have with their children when arrangements are made by the Family Courts of the UK, and significantly higher than the very best a father can expect from a Family Court Order.

Below this minimum of 33 per cent of non-school time, children become anxious and emotionally troubled by their relationship with their father. Two-thirds of children subject to this inadequate time with their fathers do not suffer any measurable effect, as this deficit is compensated for in relationships with others, such as a stepfather. However, in one-third of cases science has established that the loss of a relationship with a father is devastatingly harmful to a child. Importantly, there is no way of predicting what causes a child to fall into each of these categories – so effectively all children who are denied shared-parenting following family break-ups are at risk of harm.

Studies of the harm that results in the effected one-third of children who were given inadequate parenting time (meaning less than a third of their non-school time) with both biological parents after a family break-up indicate that they have a significantly higher risk of:

- ☹ Abuse of alcohol or drugs in childhood.
- ☹ Physical diseases, particularly of their immune or endocrine system.
- ☹ Risky early sex, and in girls a high incidence of teenage pregnancy.
- ☹ Poor educational attainment.
- ☹ Abuse/neglect by the prime/resident parent (up to a fourfold increase).
- ☹ Mental and health problems in adult life.
- ☹ Being unemployed as an adult and failing in their relationships.

Unfortunately, none of this science, which comes from America, can be used in a British Family Court. However, all of this is still worth knowing, for if you feel your offspring should have shared-parenting after a family break-up, you are right! The principle is worth fighting for as you risk damage being done to your children.

Yet, how do you argue this case?

What fathers are often faced with is not only a belief by a court that shared-parenting after separation is bad for children; it also is bad for the State. The reasoning goes that the more time apportioned to fathers with their children, the less of a claim a mother has for maintenance payments, and the more she can potentially, therefore, claim from the State. Also, the more time a father has with his children the more able he is to also claim social housing, and what is more the less time he has to work and so he too could need to claim benefits for the same children.

Every case is entirely different, there are no off-the-shelf solutions, but the best strategy to overcome this bias thinking is to address the component parts of the counter-argument, and not to tackle the whole issue head-on. I can give you a few suggestions:

You could prove that you have the resources, or shortly will, or will over time, for two acceptable family homes. That both homes are within easy reach of your children's social, family and school lives and that neither home detracts from the Welfare Checklist.

You can suggest the use of an independent private social worker — they do exist — through which messages about swap-overs can be vetted, at least on your side, so that the communication that goes with a shared-parenting arrangement is not distressing for the mother.

You can suggest that both parents attend regular sessions with a shared-parenting counsellor to iron out issues as they develop.

You may try and get an assessment report entered into the court proceedings to determine if there any signs of distress in your children from a lack of shared-parenting, or if there is a likelihood of this developing later (and so introducing the above science via the back door).

If you can find another family nearby who already have a shared-parenting arrangement and can speak about how it was at first and how it works now, they could be brought as witnesses, especially if they and their children are befriended by your family, (and organisations like Gingerbread may help to identify someone).

Finally, you need to recognise in your statement that initially shared-parenting will be hard for your kids. I know, as I have such an arrangement and for the first six months it is very difficult.

Parent alienation – as a process does not exist.

The reasoning here is that when children spend the majority of their time with one parent, following divorce or separation, they will naturally adopt many of the views of that parent. Expressing negativity about an ex-partner may be part of a necessary healing process for the resident parent, and in any event nothing can be done about such comments as they are impossible to police. Further, if a resident parent's negative comments are affecting children's attitudes to the contact parent, the solution is to remove that other parent altogether, to reduce the stress in the family as a whole. However, a negative remark made by a parent who only has visitation rights with his children, i.e. a contact parent, is viewed by a court as divisive and a means of continuing the abuse of a mother – and therefore her children.

Parent alienation as a syndrome was first proposed by a Child Psychiatrist, Richard Gardner, in several papers. He defined PAS as:

"… a disorder that arises primarily in the context of child-custody disputes. Its primary manifestation is the child's campaign of denigration against the parent, a campaign that has no justification. The disorder results from the combination of indoctrinations by the alienating parent, and a child's own contributions to the vilification of the alienated parent." [*Recent Trends in Divorce and Custody Litigation*, Academy Forum, Volume 29, Number 2, Summer, 1985].

Gardner postulated parent alienation was a measurable mental disorder and so a syndrome. However, this has been put to bed by the American Psychiatric Association who did not include this condition in the definitive work called the DSM (Diagnostic and Statistical Manual of Mental Disorders). Therefore parent alienation is not a syndrome (QED). The key distinction is that the diagnoses listed in the DSM relate to the mental health of the diagnosed individual, as opposed to attempting to describe a disorder of the relationship between different people.

However, although it is wrong to call parent alienation a syndrome, or mental disorder, PAS is a real process that is linked to the damage done to a large proportion of children denied shared-parenting following separation of their parents. The remedy other countries have found is prevention, by making sure children spend sufficient time in each of two homes, each run by one of their biological parents. Any negativity is then far more likely to rebound on the parent using PAS as the children remain bonded to each parent and each home equally. Feedback from the children will, therefore, likely cause the use of parent-alienation to cease.

A lot of fathers try to use this latter reasoning in the UK's Family Courts. They provide evidence of parent alienation by a mother and then ask a court for an order for their children to spend more time with their father, to balance things out. Yet, in the eyes of UK courts this is a ridiculous suggestion. What a court will take this proposal as saying is that the children should be forced to live at the centre of disputes between the parents, and be tortured by indoctrination on both sides.

As a result fathers who provide evidence of PAS as a means of getting a shared-parenting order are likely to paint themselves into a corner, and that corner is a No Contact Order. As thanks to the addition of Section 2B in the CA 1989, a court is able to meet the criteria of a child having the benefit of involvement of both of their parents through indirect contact. The legal test for such an order can be if the Welfare Checklist indicates a child's interests are best met by ending an intractable or destructive dispute between parents – as otherwise this dispute would go on and on, and the child would therefore suffer.

Again, every case is different and the solution to the above conundrum created by the court's misconceptions on the value of shared-parenting will need to address the particular circumstances of your life. However, I would suggest that the use of parent alienation as part of a court case needs to be handled with care. It should perhaps only be used when proposing a complete reversal of residence – with all the consequential disruption to a father's normal working life. To achieve a reversal of residence a father will probably need a series of court cases, not just the one, probably run over several years. In these hearings a father has to prove a consistent pattern of out-and-out defiance of court orders by a mother, and some resulting harm to their child or children.

In 2017, there was a break-through case: EWFC B24 (22nd March, 2017). In this case, a female Judge reversed the residence of a nine-year-old girl from her mother to her father. This judgment went against the wishes of the child and meant a change of school and home. This order was made after the mother repeatedly ignored court orders allowing a couple of hours a month of contact with the father at a contact centre. Notably, a Child Psychologist's report on the alienating effect of the mother was central. Also notable was the fact that the father lost contact with his two older children by the same mother.

A child's true wishes – are always faithfully expressed in a court through social service staff.

Courts are required to use the best authority they have for an assessment of children and other family members' lives. Judges cannot go and visit people at home, nor can they interview a child in the witness box. The Department of Justice has ordained that Cafcass or Local Authority social workers **are** the authority on assessments of families for the Family Court, and that these people have been trained in what they regard as a profession (it isn't) over many years. What is more, social workers are considered to be what is called an 'officer of the court' – so to insult them is to insult the court.

If a report from a Cafcass worker says your children have said they do not want to see you or live with you, it is no good at all to claim the social worker is not representing the wishes of your children, if the courts have no other source but you. It is further destructive to your case to claim a social worker is biased (they are), or corrupt, or a feminist, and even more detrimental to claim that they are blind to the parent alienation influence of the mother (see discussion above).

Yet, I have never seen a court shrink from ruling that a social worker's assessment be superseded by a more qualified expert on a specific issue. In my view social workers are forced on Judges, rather than their expertise being respected. For it is obvious to most that social workers are often quite dim, poorly educated and immature. The real problem is getting any other qualified opinion into a court case.

There are long-standing Practice Directives for Family Courts to do with the introduction of experts into evidence, i.e. Family Court PD 25, and these rules do not present any insurmountable obstacles. However, recent upsets in a number of Family Court cases, where mothers failed to get what they wanted as a result of the use of Child Psychologists by fathers, came to the attention of the forces mentioned in chapter nine – *How did it come to this?* This triggered a Ministry of Justice review manned by a raft of women, who fall into the category of those mentioned in chapter nine, including a Sarah J. Brown, a supposed expert on sexual violence in families. Through the mechanisms in the aforementioned chapter, a change of the Family Court rules was thus created, in 2014.

Section 13 of the new Children and Family Act 2014 now says you cannot include expert assessments as evidence unless a court has given a specific order allowing its use, regardless of the qualifications of the expert, or relevance of the expert's examination. Such changes are aimed at making it harder for fathers to introduce an expert to overrule the views of a social worker (as this mechanism was beginning to work too well)!

The use of Child Psychologists, especially when a Cafcass worker has already sided with a mother, is always opposed and with the introduction of the 2014 Law Act this opposition is now more effective. Fathers must therefore ensure the reasons for introducing experts such as Child Psychologists do not conflict with the role of social workers.

For example, it would be a bad idea to ask for the thoughts and wishes of children to be determined by a Child Psychologist. While thoughts and wishes of children are nearly always determined in a gender-bias and incompetent way — generally in a cosy chat with mother and child — the courts are not now allowed to acknowledge these failings. A better stance is one that says: 'there is a need for a whole family appraisal concerning ongoing detrimental behaviours from one or both parents'.

Allegations of domestic abuse – are no less credible because they are spoken about for the first time when they give an advantage to a mother in court.

The defence strategy of querying why an allegation of sexual or violent abuse is being made at an opportune point in time, and not mentioned at all before, has been tested in cases brought under the #MeToo virtual campaign, as well as in many Family Court hearings. This defence is usually accompanied by evidence that the accuser demonstrated affection or being happy with the accused immediately after, or before, the alleged incident. Such a defence has been tested not only with Judges, but with courts that included a jury! It is worth learning from these cases: that this sort of defence does not work.

Why? Perhaps the thinking goes that the abuse includes subjugation of the accuser, who is hoping to smooth over the abuse, for the sake of a relationship, for the sake of her children, something she desperately wants. That she is an innocent victim of violence and abuse, disbelieving of what has happened to her, feeling embarrassed and ashamed because she should have known better, trying to put the whole thing out of her mind.

Of course, the other (more probable) explanation for opportune allegations of abuse is that they are a sign of manipulation, which the accuser knows will not be punished if found out. After all, 95 per cent of rape accusers are proven, in robust court cases with a Judge and jury, to be out-and-out liars. Nothing happens to the 19 out of every 20 women who year in year out make false accusations of rape, but a hell of a lot happens to the man found innocent – who can never return to the life they had before. Such outcomes are common knowledge, and so false allegations go on unrestrained. So it is also with allegations of domestic abuse in the Family Courts, and I speak as someone who has helped women, as a McKenzie Friend, put together Witness Statements of such abuse.

Some of the finest legal minds in the world have failed to defend innocent men in court when confronted with allegations of abuse of women, so not surprisingly I do not have a watertight answer to offer. I can only suggest that a far better CDA defence-strategy is to rely on the adage that 'someone telling the truth doesn't need to have a good memory [but a liar does]'.

Firstly, I would avoid the temptation to enter a defence of CDA in writing – it nearly always ends badly. Far better to keep replies really short, such as just putting 'denied'.

Defence in advocacy should pick at the fine detail of accusations, with the court bundle for the witness kept firmly shut, to highlight inconsistencies in a false-accuser's story. I would suggest not going straight to the allegations, but instead get the accuser to give a background of the good parts of a relationship. If the witness insists the whole thing was bad this will imply she is at the very least ingenuous. If the witness accepts the good parts to the relationship's history it then makes it harder for her to paint in lies of abuse, without tripping up. However, it is a real skill to stop such recounting of events from being hijacked to stage emotions, **which can be very believable and decisive!** Also, it is tough to persistently go through the details of allegations, as a LiP-advocate facing an accuser in court, without looking abusive. Therefore, use of a barrister in a trial that includes CDA is absolutely paramount.

NB: Countering allegations of being an abuser with accusations of having been abused, (i.e. that both parties to the case were equally abusive, as is often the situation) simply does not work even if it is true. Firstly, it is an obvious ploy for a guilty person – and you will be questioned why you didn't mention the abuse before the accuser did? Secondly, a court is legally empowered to ignore one set of allegations entirely, and that set is usually about the abuse of a man (whose gender does not ordinarily attract much empathy).

NOTES ON FILLING IN YOUR C100

The application form is the instrument that gets you into court. It remains unchanged during a court case unless you apply to the court for permission to drop part of your case.

I am not going to give you a blow-by-blow, box-by-box, description of how to fill in a C100 form, but only some pointers on how to go about it. Importantly you should realise that filling in a C100 form is the last thing to do, and not the first.

A sound application means being prepared in the ways identified in the preceding chapters. It is, therefore, worth running down the following checklist to see if you are ready:

1. Is there any out-of-court agreement possible having read through chapters two and three?
2. Have you documented attempts to settle the matter out of court over a serious amount of time – at least three months (see chapter 11)?
3. Have you got the time and money for this court case, e.g. have you set a budget for a defined litigation team, or have you explored your eligibility for Legal Aid (see chapters 4, 5 and 10)?
4. Have you drafted a target court order(s) in longhand and legal terms (see chapter 11)?

5. Have you discussed the order(s) you want with a legal expert or someone else on your litigation team?

6. Have you drafted the legal argument for the above target order(s) and have you got the evidence that meets the legal test of these arguments, and if not how are you going to get this evidence (see chapter 11)?

7. Have you a clear idea, written or not, about the common-sense arguments you are going to use, and what evidence you need/have to support these arguments, bearing in mind the pitfalls of prejudice in the courts?

8. Have you a draft of your Witness Statement in support of your application? **NB: Do not send your draft Witness Statement with the C100 form**.

9. Have you attended a MIAM meeting, or are you exempt, or is the respondent claiming exemption (see chapter seven)?

10. Have you got accurate and up-to-date information on family members to be named on the C100 application form?

If you have already prepared an order you want you can put this in the application form, although you will need to reduce it down. The part that you need to reproduce on the C100 is in section 10, "The court Orders that…"

If you have sketched out your legal arguments before completing the application form, you will have a better understanding of why you need to fill in a lot of the information asked. For example, the court needs to know that you are one of the types of people listed in section 10 CA 1989 (and just saying you are is enough, until challenged) and that you have satisfied FPD 12B Section 8.4 by having attended a MIAM or have proved you are exempt. Also, what you write in the text boxes on the C100 form (and others) should show firstly, that your application is serious, as under FPD 4A applications can be struck out if they are:

```
"(a) those which set out no facts indicating what the application
is about; those which are incoherent and make no sense; those which
contain a coherent set of facts but those facts, even if true, do not
disclose any legally recognizable application against the respondent.

2.2 An application may fall within rule 4.4(1)(b) where it cannot
be justified, for example, because it is frivolous, scurrilous or
obviously ill-founded."
```

In other words, a case where a parent wants a court to decide if a child should be picked up at 4 pm or 8 pm, if this was all there was to the case, might not make it into a court as the application could be seen as frivolous. You also need to write something that helps a court decide how complex or urgent your application is, so they can allocate it to the right level of Judge and at the right time and so on. If you have done a draft of your Witness Statement, it should be a matter of cutting and pasting leading paragraphs. Whichever way you do it, be concise and make sure what you write is not open to misinterpretation.

Fill in **all** the detailed information on the parties involved in the litigation (an FPD recommends striking out those which are not done in full), for without this CAFCASS cannot do their initial checking.

On the whole, the court forms guide you through what is needed, but it is important to know why things are being asked in order to stay in control of your application. For example, a 'specific issue', as mentioned on the C100 form, is something often misunderstood. This phrase means something exact in Family Law, as defined in the CA 1989 Section 1:

"… a specific issue order means an order giving directions for the purpose of determining a specific question which has arisen, or which may arise, in connection with any aspect of parental responsibility for a child."

In other words, whether a child is picked up at 4 pm or 8 pm is a child arrangements matter, not a specific issue matter. A specific issue would be something like an order to decide which of a choice of schools a child should attend.

It is not necessary, or advisable, to accompany a C100 form with a C1A form, (which is used for allegations of abuse). The other party may wish to make use of this form in responding and it is always tempting to follow a C100 form with a C1A for this reason – but don't.

From March, 2019, a trial is being run of online applications to court, but only in some areas. This means you can fill in forms for the Family Courts, (including the C100), on your PC without needing to send anything in the post (even to the other party).

13

How to Prepare a Final Hearing Court Bundle

BUNDLE CONTENTS

This section covers tips on the content of court bundle documents, which is a separate task from the printing and production of a court bundle, as explained in the final part of this chapter. Overlapping content writing with production/printing is a terrible idea, except for last-minute changes. Solicitors usually shut down communication about a court bundle when they start producing it, usually two weeks before the target send-date, which is generally at least four days before a court hearing. For a LiP preparing a court bundle, I would close down the content one month before the print/production phase. Either way, you need to be fully MS competent and have a good computer and printer.

Notes on an index

Every page of a court bundle should be paginated. The index usually has four columns: section number, description of an item, date item was 'served' (sent), (i.e. by the court to a party(ies), or by you to someone (or vice versa)) and the page number where it can be found. All documents within a bundle section must be in date order. NB: Page numbers run sequentially across each section, but not throughout the whole bundle – this means extra pages can be added on to a section (sometimes at court) without disrupting the numbering of the entire bundle. It is best to put page numbers on the top right of the page, always in the same position, and use the nomenclature A1, A2… for section A; B1, B2, B3… for section B, and so on. A full list of sections and what should be included in each is given in Figure 4.

Preliminary documents

At the front of court bundles there are the preliminary documents which can include: Statement of Case, Case Summary, Statement of Issues, Skeleton Argument, Position Statement, Chronology, Time Estimates, and Essential Reading for the hearing.

Which preliminary documents a court wants is sometimes detailed within interim orders, but often those preparing bundles just chuck-in what they want anyway. LiPs can get hung-up on these things. Some Fathers' Support Organisations put a lot of store in producing additional documents, even for a preliminary hearing, such as a Position Statement. This is not necessary, but it can be a place to make something clear about what you want that does not stand out in standard court forms. Prelim documents in any court bundle are meant to inform, not persuade a Judge, to help him get to grips with what the case is about – and should not be in any way commentary or evidential. Reading List is a document detailed in Practice Directions but in fact is not put in most bundles as this is given at the end of a hearing as a Judge rises to take time out to come to their decision.

Bundle Index
A. **Preliminary Documents** e.g.
  Statement of Case (optional, normally a device for a barrister)
  Statement of Issues (as above)
  Chronology
  Position Statement for Final Hearing – Applicant
  Position Statement for Final Hearing – Respondent
  Finding of Facts – a marked-up Scott Schedule
  Applicant's Reading List – Final Hearing (optional)
  Respondent's Reading List – Final Hearing (optional)
B. **Applications and Orders**
C. **Statements & Affidavits**
D. **Care Plans**
E. **Expert Reports**
F. **Miscellaneous Documents** e.g.
  Exhibit A to the Applicant's 1st Witness Statement
  Exhibit B to the Applicant's 1st Witness Statement
  Exhibit A to Respondent's Witness Statement
  School Report
  Character Reference for Applicant
  Respondent's Position Statement for Fact-Finding Hearing
  Judge XXX's written findings from Fact-Finding Hearing
  Anon…

Figure 4. Court Bundle headings prescribed under Family Law Practice Direction 27A.

Chronology

One strand in a Witness Statement is the timeline. However else you describe events, and detail reasons for you having your desired order, time is always there. A Chronology is one of the preliminary documents that I advise always using from the outset of a court case.

At first, you may not be able to think of much to put on a timeline, such as: got married, had children, split-up, argued, applied to court. Yet, as you think about things and work through your Witness Statement, more things can usually be added by going back and forth from the timeline, or Chronology, to your draft statement. You may also find a Chronology very useful in dissecting the respondent's argument. For example, to tell if you are describing the same event as the respondent, but differently, or describing two separate incidents, or whether you or they have got the order of events wrong.

Chronologies are limited to ten A4 sheets. They usually consist of a list of items in three columns: date, a short one to four word description of an event and whether the parties agree with an event or not. If a Scott Schedule is also produced the allegations in that schedule should be cross-referenced to this Chronology document.

Skeleton Argument

A document that teases out the core of an argument that one party is advancing is called a Skeleton Argument, (mandatory in an Appeal Court Hearing application). Along with a chronology this can be a highly useful tool to sketch out your case before drafting a Witness Statement (see prior chapters), even if you later do not include it in the court bundle.

Case Summary/Statement of Case/Time Estimates

A Statement of Case sets out the whole picture of a case, including the known facts (as you understand them), what your application is about, the reasons for it, as well as describing the respondent's counter-application. A Statement of Case may refer to relevant law, but its primary aim is to set out the facts of your case and not present a legal argument. Facts must be clear, concise and not contradictory. A Statement of Case may also include details of witnesses on whom you intend to rely. This sort of document is meant to help a Judge anticipated the time needed to deal with the issues in a case, and is best when written by a barrister. A Case Summary document, if you chose to produce one, is limited to six A4 sides of paper.

Statement of Issues

This is a technical document that objectively informs a Judge what the case is about, and is limited to two A4 sheets. What may appear as issues in a common-sense way may not be an issue at all in law, for example, because the law compels a Judge to behave in a way you don't want. If you are using a direct access barrister, you can get him/her to prepare this document (and a barrister may consider it unnecessary).

Issues need to be split into issues for this hearing, and issues for the Final Hearing. Unless the case is complicated, for example the matter is returning to court from a previous hearing, this document is not normally used in a first hearing. 'Issues' are usually quite apparent to a court from the content of application forms and the responses of the other party.

The sort of thing a Family Court normally considers as issues are:

- What the couple are arguing about with respect to child arrangements, i.e. what the essential points of disagreement are, as opposed to things they do agree on.

- A court will consider if a couple in a case can be persuaded to reach an agreement on the issues of disagreement, and have an order made by consent. If you think a deal is possible at court, this is an issue. If an agreement is not possible, it is not an issue.

- A court will consider whether making an order is better than not making an order given the types of order a court can make and its powers to enforce them. If it is clear what you want as an order, and how it is possible to be implemented in law, and if it is clear this will make things better, this is not an issue. If it is unclear what order you want, or if it is unclear how a court can make the order you want, or if it is unclear how such an order will help, these are all issues.

- An issue can be whether a child under 16-years-old can competently understand the things disputed and can express his/her wishes, (what is known as being Gillick Competent). If the child is of the right age, it can be an issue of how these wishes can be captured and recorded. If the child is too young or has no wishes, then this is not an issue. If the child is old enough and has a view, and you want the child's wishes ascertained in a certain way, and disagree with the other party with this method, then these become issues.

- ☯ If the outcome of CAFCASS' investigations are known and Social Services, CAFCASS, or the Welsh equivalent, have no concerns, then this is not an issue. If you don't know the outcome of these investigations, or if CAFCASS have concerns, then this is always an issue.

- ☯ Alleged domestic abuse is usually taken as an issue. This issue can be split into several sub-issues: whether the claimed abuse is prima facia ridiculous, or on the face of it possible. If the allegations are deemed possible, that abuse occurred, it is then an issue if these claims are something that can be determined by a Fact-Finding Hearing, or by an expert report of some sort – and such a report needs to be around something specific, not a general investigation. Unless someone makes outrageous or trivial claims (e.g. he always hides the biscuits), claims of abuse normally are an issue at the first hearing.

Any other activities a court could order, or direct, that would narrow down the points of disagreement between a couple are also issues for a court hearing, and these should be put in this document.

Position Statement

A Position Statement is something that should be rewritten each time there is a hearing. It is a summary of your litigation, with reasons and background to the case, as well as what orders you want the court to make at the next and the Final Hearing. A Position Statement, therefore, repeats the application form to some extent. However, as a court case progresses, and information and evidence changes your opinion of what you want or will get, so you might want to change the detail of the order you want. The document is limited to three A4 sides of paper.

Like other preliminary documents produced at court hearings a Position Statement's primary purpose is to inform a Judge of what the case is about but, of course, in so doing you are also trying to convince him. For apart from anything else the Judge needs to make decisions in interim hearings on what further steps are needed before the Final Hearing and you need these steps to support your argument for the order you want. In the Final Hearing the Position Statement, in my view, becomes far less important as by then the court will have your entire Witness Statement – your main document in the court case.

In detail, a Position Statement should include some of these key points:

1. Who each of the parties are and their relationship one to another.
2. What is your relationship to the children? What is the other party's relationship to the children?
3. If you are the applicant and this is the first hearing – what has caused you to make the application?
4. Have you tried to negotiate?
5. Are you able to communicate with the other party?
6. Has there been domestic violence to your children from the other party?
7. What has happened since the last hearing or court case on this same matter (for example, documents you have sent to the court, documents you have received from the other party, any documents the other party was supposed to send to you which you have not received)?

8. If you have not complied with any Court Directions then provide a short explanation why not.
9. Any Court Directions that the other party has failed to comply with.
10. What directions do you want the court to make at the hearing?
11. What order do you want?
12. Do your children have any special needs?
13. Do you want permission to file any further evidence, if so, what sort of evidence?

Applications and Orders

This section of a court bundle contains a copy of each application form sent by either party and every order or direction issued by any Judge in the case, including notices of hearings sent from the Court Office. It is not a place to put emails and letters to and from the court, or to and from the other party. Copies of these applications and orders have to be numbered and arranged in date-sent order. If you do not have a particular form used by the other side, you can mark it as missing, except in the Final Hearing court bundle (unless you are making the point about someone disobeying Court Directions). Make sure the orders in this section are copies of the final version, and not drafts.

Statement and Affidavits

Usually documents in this section are put in groups, the applicant's first and then the respondent's. These cannot be letters, emails and other documents in which people have made statements, but only official documents of a certain structure as defined in Practice Direction 27A. Usually, in Child Arrangement Cases, there is only one statement from each party, unless there has been a Fact-Finding Hearing. Although Fact-Finding Statements are no longer of much use in a Final Hearing, as facts will have been found, these statements should also be put in this section — and as a rule of thumb any document sent to the court stays within the bundle to the end of a court case. It is permissible, with the permission of the court, to submit many statements into the one case, but each statement must use 12-11 point-size font, with 1.5 line-spacing, and be no more than 25 A4 pages long.

Care Plans and Expert Reports

An example of a Care Plan is a Social Services Parenting Plan. A Section 7 report and Safeguarding Letter/Report are examples of Expert Reports. Only reports that have been generated through the Family Court Expert Report process can be included here. This means they must have been agreed by a court and the contents commissioned by a jointly agreed letter from both parties, unless the reports have been ordered by the Judge for his own reasons or on the recommendation of CAFCASS. Police Reports are usually put as attachments to either an Expert Report or a Witness Statement and are not Expert Reports in themselves.

Miscellaneous documents

Things that normally go in Section F are: a) certificate/notice of other proceedings that are going on at the same time and relate to this court hearing; b) Notice of Wardship of a child; c) Notice of Acting from a solicitor (although if there is a solicitor you should not be preparing this bundle); d) Notice of Legal Aid (and again this implies a solicitor and so you should not be doing this bundle); e) any evidence attached to a C1A form claiming violence or abuse.

Things that cannot be included in any bundle without the permission of the court are: i) correspondence (including letters of instruction to experts); ii) medical records (including hospital, GP and health visitor records); iii) bank and credit card statements and other financial records; iv) notes of contact visits; v) foster carer logs; vi) social services files (except for any assessment being relied on by any of the parties); vii) police disclosures.

If you want to include authorities such as Scientific Research or Case Histories, these need to be put in a separate bundle and should be limited to 10 in number. There are rules about how Case Histories can be included in this separate bundle, (see rule 27A, Section 4.3 A.1-2).

BUNDLE PRODUCTION

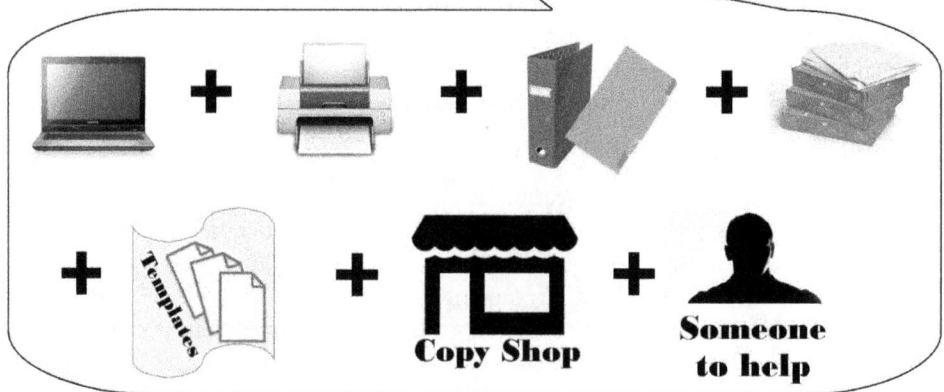

If it has fallen to you to prepare a whole court bundle and you want to do it properly, you are going to need a good printer, (preferably a laser printer). You will also need a good computer, (don't try and do it with a tablet), a few reams of A4 paper, lever arch files (bundle sizes are limited to about 380 pages per file), court document templates (or create these yourself) and access to a copy shop. Most importantly, this is not something to be done without someone to help and check things before sending.

Step 1. Check if the other side has a lawyer by phoning the Court Office and asking if any solicitor is 'on the record' for your case (NB: If there is no one 'on the record' it does not mean the other side will not be represented in court, for example, by using a last-minute appointment). If yes, go to step 11, otherwise go to step 2. Read and follow the Court Orders for any instructions/timetable for the production and exchange of different documents in the court bundle.

Step 2. One month before the court bundle is due finish all of its content.

Step 3. Print two copies of the index page and one of every other page (this creates the master copy).

Step 4. Collate your printed documents together in the order given in the index. Do not number the pages, nor enter page numbers in the index, at this stage. Do not put any documents in the bundle that are not listed in the index.

Step 5. Get a loose paper copy made of your bundle, or an electronic copy by scanning each page, by your copy shop (this is a first copy of the master copy). Send this first copy to your helper for a review and send one copy of the index page (**only the index page**) to the other party, by registered post, asking for comment (and give a deadline for this comment).

Step 6. Review the comments made by your helper and make amendments accordingly. Review the comments made by the other party for additions or extractions from the bundle and decide whether you agree with them. You need to write to the other party telling them whether you accept or reject their requests, with reasons. It is normal to agree with additions or extractions unless they are asking for something that has not been ordered by the court or is not listed in the standard index. If they ask for something to be put in that you do not have then give them a deadline to send it to you (a day or so) and say if they miss the deadline you will leave it out. If the other side says you haven't given them a document listed in the index, and you haven't, send a copy to them but give them a deadline to comment on this missing document.

Step 7. Print off or copy any new documents or changes to existing ones found in step 6. Collate these documents into a bundle following the new index order. If you are still expecting new documents which have not yet arrived from the other party, list these at the end of a section in the bundle index (remember, pages are numbered sequentially only within a section and not across the whole bundle). Put cardboard spaces between sections and put all the documents in one or more A4 lever-arch files, or 2-inch files, (depending on the volume of paper). Number all pages by hand/pencil. Fill in the index page numbers accordingly (in MS Word), then reprint two copies of the index with the page numbers included.

Step 8. Have a copy shop make three copies of your master bundle. Send the index page, with page numbers, to the other party no less than four days before the final hearing.

Step 9. No later than two days before the hearing provide a paginated copy of the bundle to the Court Office (remembering to follow any timetable in the Court Orders that are in your case). If you want to protect your strategy, all the preliminary documents, apart from the Chronology, can be held back until the day of the hearing (in which case you need four copies of these to take to the court on the day of the hearing).

Step 10. In the court building, or shortly beforehand, (it is up to you), give a copy of the bundle to the other party, and give an extra copy to the courtroom clerk for witnesses to use in the witness box (if this is the main hearing).

Step 11. If the other side is preparing the bundle, for example, if they are the ones who have a lawyer but you do not, ask to see the index at least three weeks before the hearing or as dictated in any Preliminary Court Order(s). If you are ignored, which often happens, start at step 1 and create your own bundle. If the other side does send you an index, check to see if there any documents not listed that you want to be included. Write to ask these be included, but at the same time start to prepare a supplementary bundle, (by editing the index and going through steps 5–10 in preparing this bundle). At court have four copies of this supplement to give out, if needed, after first clearing this action with the court.

14

What if you Lose?

"... grant me the courage to change the things I can, serenity to accept the things I cannot change, and wisdom to know the difference." Niebuhr, Reinhold. [A version of the *Serenity Prayer*; attributed to Reinhold, composed around 1932-33].

I can tell you that you won't find the answer to the above question at the bottom of a glass. Also, the hard truth is that nobody likes a loser.

Before your court case, most people you know may have sympathised with your situation and wished you luck in getting it sorted out in the courts. Yet once you have been weighed and measured, and found lacking, few have any compassion. There will be an unnavigable chasm between you and others, none of whom have likely suffered outright injustice, or had their children kidnapped. People will want you to just get on with your life, bereft of your kids. Do not expect any mercy from the other party either. During the court case they may have, at the very least, felt glad that what was being done to you was not being done to them. Yet, however inhuman the stripping of your fatherhood may self-evidently be, a verdict empowers a victor and they will from then on be even less inclined to compromise or give ground. If perceptive, a mother will also realise that the Court Order is there for you to obey, but not her.

At least, it should now be clear to you what all the noise was about when people said, "Stay away from the Family Courts."

Before, you were probably prevented from parenting your children by their absence, being kept behind locked doors or at school, maybe with a few interventions from the police. Now you have a Court Order against you things are many times worse.

It is hardly surprising that the first thing most want if they receive a child arrangement order that undermines them as a father is to 'do the court case all over again', what is often referred to by laypeople as an appeal. Sadly, what you first have to come to terms with is that redoing a court case is not an appeal and that a court case can **never** be run twice.

The subject of recourse for a lousy judgment becomes complicated very quickly, with the option of not using a legal expert void – you will always need a lawyer. The processes of a statutory appeal are mainly outside the scope of this book and require an enormous amount of effort and money in a very short space of time. However, although lawyers can give you many options, to me the choices are few. I would simplify things down to the following.

Post-Final Hearing you have a fork in your path. You can wait probably about two to three years, and run another court case in the Lower Courts. Or you can immediately appeal the order of the Lower Court Hearing to the next highest court. In theory Family Appeal Courts are three-tiered: County Court, High Court and Supreme Court.

A LEGAL APPEAL

The tiers of Appellate Courts for the Family Division are to me academic. In reality, if you started at the Magistrate level, a County Court will usually rubber-stamp a Lower Court's decision, with a single Judge hearing and rejecting an appeal, or refusing it on sight of the papers. Only an appeal in the Family Division High Court can make a difference, where a panel of three Judges sits in adjudication. However, the High Court will not hear an appeal until the Lower Courts have done their stuff. There is also the right to appeal to the Supreme Court, but this is a court who decides things such as, in 2019, if Parliament was prorogued. With a panel of 12 Judges, it would be rare indeed for a Family Court Order to find its way to an Appeal Hearing there. What is more, Lady Hale sits in this court so it would be a waste of time anyway.

Appellate Courts do not reconsider the evidence heard in a preceding court case, and they will not rehear witnesses. What they mostly do is adjudicate on errors in the processes used. Yet, they will only do this if on the surface of an application it seems the appellant, or the pursuer in Scotland, has a sound legal argument to be considered. This is decided in a pre-hearing evaluation which is done in one of two ways: in writing, or in writing followed by a short 20-minute hearing. If a High Court Appeal refuses your application after this evaluation, or hears the appeal but rejects it, you are then, realistically, stuck with your existing Lower Court Order for life and have to live with it.

The starting point of an appeal is always in the court you just left. There you have to ask the Judge, immediately after he pronounces an order that you do not want, for permission to appeal. Preferably you should also ask for a written explanation of why he refuses your appeal as this will help your application to the Appellate Courts. The Judge may, in return, ask the grounds you intend to use to appeal.

This procedural step is often missed by fathers and can cause an appeal application to fall apart before it starts. For if you forgot to ask a Judge for permission to appeal, the time it takes to get this documented after a Final Hearing could mean your application times-out. Now for the big shocker, the time limit for lodging an appeal (with all Appeal Bundle documents completed) is 21 days from the date of your Lower Court Final Hearing!

The filtering of cases into the Appellate Courts is very severe. Only 30–50 High Court Civil Appeals are heard each year, and some put the percentage of those being granted permission at one to two per cent of all applications. What you also have to grasp, quite apart from the whirlwind process of an appeal, is that an Appellate Court is likely only to do one of two things. They may alter some details in the existing order, (but not change it substantially) or they will set the order aside, for the case to be heard a second time in the Lower Courts. In other words, if you are successful in being granted an appeal, and win that appeal, there is yet another step of having your case reheard, and there you have to win all over again.

A chief parameter you need to be mindful of here is time. Appeal applications are evaluated quickly, but getting an Appeal Court Hearing takes around six months and then getting to a Lower Court FHDRA afterwards would be at least another six to nine months. Then that court case would take a further nine months. As a consequence, any second Family Court trial would not be the same as the one you lost. Maybe two or three years will have past. All the evidence will therefore be different, especially the assessment of your children's wishes – and usually this changes in favour of a mother as by then your offspring may have de-bonded from you as a father. What is more, unbelievably, you can be told to have the case reheard by the same Judge as before!

Knowing the types of issues that can lead to the granting of permission to appeal is a black art. Nobody knows. We are dealing with a real 'will of the King' scenario (as discussed in chapter two). A person who might be able to guess better than most is someone who spends a lot of time in the presence of High Court Judges, in other words, a barrister. Consulting this type of person is a good starting point and **not** Form FP161, as most fathers seem to think. So, to commence an appeal first take a rough draft of an Appeal Court bundle — constructed along the lines of the practice directions for an appeal — and pay a barrister for a legal opinion on the chances of being granted an Appeal Hearing.

At this point, I can throw you a bone. It is more probable you will pass the Legal Aid Agency's merits test for an Appeal Case, than for a Lower Family Court case, (especially if you pass the Appeal Court's initial appraisal). Even before you reach the Appeal Court's appraisal stage, you can approach a solicitor for Legal Help, for example, to cover the costs of a discussion about the merits of your appeal case, as Legal Help is something a solicitor can authorise themselves. If you subsequently, off your own bat, get a favourable legal opinion on the merits of an appeal from a barrister, (regardless of what the solicitor thinks) then you automatically enter the appeal process with Legal Aid backing. This backing can then be rolled over to fund your entire appeal – and subsequent retrial if you win the appeal. What is more, as the appeal process happens so quickly, there will be none of the usual delays in the Agency releasing tranches of funding for various steps in the court process, and the funding a solicitor will get is better than in many other court cases.

So what sort of case is likely to win an appeal?

I can give you examples of two Family Division High Court Appeals I have won with clients, but I do not have the answer to the above question, and I would be wary of anyone who says they do. You should also be warned that the appeal process invites the other party in the Lower Court case to come and knock lumps out of your argument. However, sweetness of sweetness, Legal Aid funding can become reversed at this point. A mother Legally Aided at a Lower Court hearing, because of CDA, will not be funded as a respondent in the Appeal Court case, even though a father may be funded.

In one appeal to the High Court, my client had tried to counter accusations of mental instability, being the reason he had allegedly abused his ex, by getting a psychiatric assessment to prove he was sane. He had gone to a clinical psychiatrist and University Lecturer who made a good side-income from court appearances. The psychiatrist's assessment consisted of a 20-minute chat, at a cost of £1,500, from which the psychiatrist wrote a letter saying he thought my client suffered from a personality disorder.

Of course, my client did not submit this report, which had not been done with the permission of the court anyway. I was not surprised by what had happened, not because my client did have a personality disorder, but because of the strain he was under from a two-year court case. He had started to fight fire with fire, (a common mistake fathers make). As part of this my client embellished wrongdoing by the other party, saying he had been abused by his ex, to a point where, just like most purveyors of CDA, he had begun to believe his own fiction. I got to know my client's thinking. In his mind, I could see that he believed that as long as there was truth somewhere in his statements, the means justified the ends, even if this meant exaggerations and lies. He was, after all, facing a continuation of a No Contact Order with his child.

What my client was unaware of was that without the mantle of victimhood (that mothers have) his embellishments made his accusations fantastic, even if in part they were real. Presented with a series of tall-tales from my client, the psychiatrist knew that standard tests for an abnormal mental state would be pointless. However, personality disorders are from a special pseudo-science. This makes the proposition that if many bad things befall a person, even though that person is normal on mental-health scales, in some part that person's behaviour must be responsible for the disasters. It is a sort of self-fulfilling diagnosis. Of course, my client's exaggerated stories seemed to the doctor proof of many disastrous incidents and therefore, proof of a personality disorder. It was simply a misdiagnosis.

When my client lost his court case in a way that made things worse for him, with Prohibitive Steps Orders added to an existing No Contact Order, he asked me for help in appealing to the High Court in the Royal Courts of Justice. The case I helped him put together was based on a section of the CA 1989 that talked about the legal test for a party to be competent as a LiP.

In the Lower Court case my client had initially been Legal Aid funded in his application, but had subsequently fallen out with his solicitor over some social media postings he had used to try and reach out to his child. In the end, the solicitor firm refused to send a barrister to represent him at his Final Hearing. At court, my client had to represent himself, as a LiP-Advocate. However, there was a mini-hearing before the main hearing. At this hearing a barrister from the firm of solicitors my client had been using, asked permission for the solicitors to withdraw from the proceedings, and my client opposed this application.

I managed to get a letter from the original psychiatrist that clearly stated that the father was unfit to represent himself in any court hearing, according to an assessment he had done before the Final Hearing in the Lower Court case. This simple two-sentence letter, when combined with the father's insistence at the time of the Final Hearing that he needed to be represented, led to a successful appeal. It should be noted that not having a barrister, and insisting you need one, or being forced into representing yourself at a moment's notice, or claiming you are legally incompetent to represent yourself, are all arguments that have been tested in High Court Appeals and have failed. However, the exact sequence of events in the above case, together with a well-written application and legal argument referencing the precise section of the right Law Act, won the day. The result was the Lower Court Order was set aside, and the court case was ordered to be rerun.

The father, however, never reran the Lower Court case (after ten years he had had enough). Instead, he continued in his attempts to contact his child within the constraints of his No Contact Order, but without fear of arrest for breaching a Prohibitive Steps Order. Yet, the child did not respond, and shortly after the appeal case his child fell victim to one of the effects known to be attributable to a lack of shared-parenting. Today the child completely spurns the father, alienated from him for life by the lies of her mother, and lives a sad life as an unmarried teenage-mother.

In another appeal, a British father split from his British wife in a different country. The mother went back to the UK and left my client to look after their son. The father was given custody of his boy in the foreign country, and brought him up alone, save for visits to the mother in school holidays. When the mother remarried and had another child, she wanted to reunite her family. A campaign of disruption then ensued with several court actions being taken by her in the foreign Family Courts. The consequence of this was unexpected by both parties as the Foreign Family Court ordered the child to be taken into public care until both parties cooled down.

Determined not to let his child be fostered out, the father immediately took his son back to the UK. This act triggered a UK Family Court case with the mother as the applicant, shortly after joined by the Local Authority which became the guardian of the child in the case. The father tried to conduct an emotional and passionate defence completely on his own. Yet, the court processes so completely overawed him, he ended up being thrown out of the court building and the trial continued without him. As a result the Lower Family Court was misled into believing the father was a fugitive of a Foreign Family Court Order, against him alone, (which is what the mother told social services). As the child was in the UK the mother said she was willing to assume sole residency of her son. As a result, the father's five-year-old Custody Order was overturned in the UK. In its place he was given a UK No Contact Order and the mother a Sole-Residency Order, with the child sent to live with her and her new husband.

I helped launch his appeal based on what was said in letters exchanged between a Judge in the foreign country and the Court Office of the Family Court in the UK. There is a prescribed process for such transfers of what is called jurisdiction, and this process was not done correctly. The key was that the foreign Judge had said she was happy for the boy to be with her mother in the UK, (predicting the outcome of the Family Court case) which is not the same as saying she was transferring jurisdiction. An attempt was also made to launch a further argument based on the fact there existed three Family Court Orders: an order of custody for the father in a foreign country (that still had jurisdiction), an order of a Lower Court in the foreign country stating that the child should be taken into care for a period of one year, and an order of the UK Family Court (contradicting the foreign court orders). I tried to argue that if the appeal was granted, not only should the UK order be set aside, the order of the foreign Family Court should then be applied, as the care-order had expired (for it was more than one year since it was issued).

However, my client had followed my advice and instructed a direct access barrister, and he refused to use my argument (as he deemed it unworkable). As a result, the appeal was won, and the UK Family Court Order was removed, **but** the boy remained with the mother until the father reapplied for custody in either the foreign or UK courts.

The father did try to redo the court case in his home country, but that court disagreed with the UK High Court and claimed they had already transferred jurisdiction to where the child now lived, and therefore there was no possibility of another court case. Unfortunately, in the UK things had become very heated when the father's son had been ripped out of his hands. As a result, the father had been charged with contempt of court, a hearing the father did not bother to attend, and so a UK arrest warrant had been issued against him.

Faced with possible imprisonment in the UK, (albeit for a short period), and no way of starting a court case in his home country, the father accepted the situation despite having won an appeal to get his son back. Lately, I understand he received a social internet-posting that effectively said how much his son hated him.

As I said at the beginning, the most important parameter to consider in an appeal is time. For an appeal can go on for so long it effectively times-you-out as a parent. One way this happens is through the powerfully destructive tool of parent alienation. Sadly, human nature being what it is, the longer a court procedure goes on the more thoroughly this tool will be implemented by whoever it is that has 'legal residence' of the children.

RE-APPLYING TO THE LOWER FAMILY COURTS

Once an order of a Lower Family Court has been given no court is likely to move things on without a substantial change of circumstances. Attempts to apply for a new order without such changes are usually swiftly met with a 9114 or Barring Order, meant to protect a respondent from repeated applications without merit.

I cannot emphasise enough how difficult it is to get a new Family Court Order. As an example, one client of mine was subject to a No Contact Order mainly because of the strong opposition of a new stepfather, backed by the mother of his child. The mother had married after splitting with the father to set up in a new family that produced two new half-brothers. The applicant-father separated from the mother when his daughter was very young, and so his child did not know him as her real father. The argument the court accepted was that as the married couple and the estranged father were hostile to one another, the child was better off in a new stable family without any direct contact with her biological father. The new couple insisted that the biological father was liable to kidnap his child abroad, and they also successfully claimed he had been abusive to the mother.

The father, who was a well-educated professional in a new stable marriage, brought his child arrangement case back to court because of the following change of circumstances. The mother was divorcing the stepfather, who was making preparations to work abroad in what later proved to be a brothel. The mother had started working in the sex industry, including online pornography and escort work – of which the father had ample and graphic pictorial evidence. The mother had abandoned all three of her children, the eldest by the applicant, for two weeks, while she went on a holiday with a sugar daddy 34 years her senior, (which trip included her getting a boob job). While abroad social services had been called, and as a result, the family was placed under observation and special help. The school had contacted the applicant-father, as the mother and stepfather were nowhere to be found, after the father's child had been expelled for sexually assaulting another pupil and for out-of-school parties involving drugs.

None of the above facts had the slightest weight in the new Lower Family Court case. Social services rallied around the mother, who claimed the children had not been abandoned but left in the charge of a 17-year-old stranger. The mother agreed to family counselling, and brought in the children's grandfather to look after her kids while she continued to work as an escort (a job she denied despite online postings to this effect). The stepfather initially helped the applicant-father in his case, but withdrew his support when the mother threatened to cut him off from his two kids as well.

The result of the court case was that the existing Family Court Order was made more severe against the applicant-father, so that the mother, vulnerable after her divorce, was not again unduly distressed by another application.

If you lose your application to the Family Courts for a child arrangement order you know your children need, and if there is no sense in an appeal, you have to face facts that the order given is final. **The only route for recourse has already been discussed** in chapter six (under the section on *Orders*). Namely, you should have built in to the order options to come back to court, via Activity Directions, six-monthly reviews or any other mechanisms. For example, if contact between a father and his children is limited due to the father taking drugs or being violent this should be readdressed after a period of rehabilitation, and this should be part of the Final Order. If this sort of inclusion is missed out getting a later change through the Lower Family Courts of the UK is like pushing water uphill.

However, if you nonetheless want to try to reapply for a new Child Arrangement Order, then simply go back to chapter two. There are no shortcuts for a second court case.

What about enforcement?

Many fathers leap at any breach of an order by their ex as an opportunity to have their child arrangements order reassessed. Every case is different, and this could happen. However, what is more likely is for a father to finally realise that the courts produce only one winner. What a father may have thought was the court giving him some right to parent his children often turns out to be mere window dressing. For rather than punishing a mother who does not stick to an order most courts try to alter things so that she is more likely to comply in the future, by basically giving her more of what she wants. I refer you back to chapter two, and the statement that no one is going to put a mother in jail for breaking a Civil Court Order.

In many ways, it is sometimes better to roll with the punches and let things slide while keeping notes (to use at the right time). It is possible, however, to claim compensation, for instance, if a mother unreasonably cancels a holiday by holding her children back from going at the last minute. A community order may sometimes be given against a mother if repeated breaches of a Family Court Order are blatant (clearly documented and proven) and unrepentant. It has also proven possible, via a Lower Court case then an appeal, to reverse a Court Order for residence if the behaviour of a mother in breaking a Family Court Order directly and clearly harms a child – if backed by a statement from social services, an expert, or a child over the age of 14 years old (and preferably all three).

However, what is also true is that a court will not use transgressions by a mother as justification for imposing something on her children that in a prior court case was deemed unsafe. Unfortunately, many applications by fathers for enforcement **and** adjustment of an existing Family Court Order fall into this last category.

Enforcement applications follow a different route in the Family Court and start with form C79 (**see Appendix IV for how to get the form**). You will be surprised how slowly these applications are dealt with by the courts when compared to the treatment of Family Act 1996 Injunction Applications. You should be prepared to bring to court the entire court bundle for the Final Hearing of the case from where the order that has been broken originated (and be mindful that courts do not keep court bundles that are more than five years old – although firms of solicitors do). Be aware: if the other party corrects, at the last minute, something disobeyed in a Court Order, even though it is late, for example, a picture or report you are due, then there will not be much of a case to be heard.

Enforcement applications that are wrongfully brought to court, unlike most Child Arrangement Applications, can attract an order for costs against the applicant. This practice means if you applied for enforcement, but there was nothing to enforce, (as the breach either did not happen or was trivial), you pay the other party's legal costs as restitution for unnecessarily inconveniencing them. A lot of gamesmanship typically occurs in court around these last points.

15

What to do when there is No Contact

This chapter is the hardest and most contentious one to write. I will be upfront: British society treats fathers with No Contact Orders, or who are separated from their offspring by a mother, as modern-day lepers for whom there is no sympathy anywhere. What is more, everything a father fears will happen, as a result of having contact severed, probably will occur.

If your ex is preventing you see your children at all, the first thing I advise is to consider carefully if you fall into the category of 'no contact' or whether you are in what the American courts call a 'high conflict separation'. Many women will remove all contact between father and child during a post-separation drama, unfairly and cruelly, but with an endpoint. Taking drastic action over something that could potentially be resolved with a little patience would be the worst mistake you ever make.

On the other hand, I also have to caution against the opposite situation. Many men feel that over time their ex will relent and let them see their children, when in fact they simply haven't come to terms with the infamy of what the mother of their children is inflicting. Such men are then led to waste a good deal of effort and money in pointless court cases that drag on for years, as by the time they realise their ex is determined to eliminate them as a father their children have already been alienated from them, for life.

Deciding the intention of your ex-wife or partner is something only you can do. If you are only facing a difficult dispute over child arrangements, rather than a real and final application for no contact, you should start again at chapter one. If you do truthfully fall into the category of someone whose former spouse is determined that you never again see your children, my second piece of advice is about survival: **no self-pity!** Tragic as what is happening to you is, it has already happened to millions of other fathers in Great Britain before you – unseen and ignored. This occurrence is so common it has become part of Britain's contemporary culture.

SOPHIE'S CHOICE

Faced with the unthinkable, of children losing one of their parents, most fathers will usually try every other option first. After becoming frustrated and exhausted by the ineffectiveness and complexity of soft solutions, in a state of despair, they then confront the hard choice of who is to be the parent that raises their children without the other, and who it is that will make that choice – the father or the State. For the moment a modern mother becomes determined to remove the father of her children from then on those kids will only ever have one parent. The other may remain known, but only as a distant relative.

A father separated by his ex from all contact with his children is like a man at a crossroads of three roads. Imagine each of these routes fenced in, topped by barbed wire, and with ferocious animals roaming the in-between spaces. Also imagine each of these paths is dynamited behind a man once he passes down it. For if a father decides he has made a mistake there is no switching of ways. The choice he makes at this point is final.

Down one road a father can decide to let the mother be the one parent for his children, in which case he needs just to walk away and let go. If, after a while, the father realises he cannot live without his children, and that his heart is breaking, it will be to no avail at all. Family Courts have little will or power over determined, sole-resident mothers who defy Family Court orders, especially when the father did not initially want to fight for his parenthood.

Another path is a rocky and expensive one, involving a series of contested hearings in the Family Courts – about which the majority of this book advises. The **only way** a father can reach his destination on this road is to reverse the residence of his children. This may be by the skilful running of a court case or, preferably, by some physical (but legal) means before a court case starts. Only then can the powers of the courts overcome a determined mother out to erase all memory of a father.

The third and final route a father facing no contact can take means becoming an outlaw – at least in this country. If you delay in taking this path you can never cut back to it. For it is one thing to relocate a child with whom you live, but a whole different matter to abduct your child in defiance of a Family Court Order – something that can lead to a Red Listed International Arrest Warrant being issued against you.

In amongst all of these decisions there is something else to contend with, something frequently overlooked, i.e. children are not adults! Children feel differently; children remember differently. What this means is that while an adult can love in the absence of everyday contact with the object of their love, with children time is against you. Children **can** forget their parents, and stop loving them, if those parents do not spend enough time with them – a terrible thing to say but something that is nevertheless true. Of course, whether this occurs, or to what extent, depends on many factors, for example: the age of a child, the relationship of a child with a parent before separation, the personality and developmental stage of the child, the availability of parent substitutes and the emotional reaction of the remaining parent to the absent parent.

Instinctively we all know that the younger a child is the more readily and quickly they can forget a parent. Toddlers of 12 to 18 months will forget their mother and father after about six weeks, and happily latch onto a replacement. This observation is backed by a bit of science as before the 'Piaget 18-months Watershed' babies and toddlers cannot grasp permanence, so when something leaves their sight or sound to them it no longer exists at all – hence why babies' cries are so very plaintive. Below three or four years old there is another known phenomenon called 'Childhood Amnesia', (which has been talked about by psychologists since the beginning of the 1900s). This refers to the earliest childhood memories an adult can have. Recent studies indicate that Childhood Amnesia can start as late as seven years old, and occurs through a process of gradual fading of memories as a child grows past the cut off age, rather than it being a sudden loss of memory or sudden awakening of memory capabilities.

One study found that children aged between five and seven years old remembered 60 per cent of early-life events whereas older children, up to nine years old, remembered only 40 per cent of these same early-years' events (21). Most interestingly, in the same study, it was found that a mother's interaction with her child was significant in this process. When a mother encouraged discussion about a person or event, asking their children to express themselves in open-ended ways, the Childhood Amnesia effect was less, and the onset age became lower. In other words, if a mother (of children up to seven years old) blanks discussion about an adult, (even without saying anything negative), this significantly speeds a child to forget an estranged parent.

Individuals differ, but in the case of those older than seven years old it is commonly held that it can take up to two years of absence to break down feelings of attachment for a parent completely. Welfare agencies have always worked on the principle that a child left in care should not be contacted by its parents for three months, after which time he or she will not be distressed at a parent coming and going. Other studies have made it clear that for older children the negativity of a mother, in any discussion about an absent parent, significantly increases the speed of de-bonding of that child with their father.

In other words, for a child less than 18 months, separation from a parent is catastrophic after only a few weeks. For a child between two and seven years old separation over the critical Child Amnesia age can also be catastrophic, and likely to be permanently damaging if separation from a parent is over a year. For children over seven years old, perhaps all the way to a teenager, separation of two years may be needed to completely de-bond a child from a father, **but** this process can be greatly speeded-up by a mother engaging in 'parent alienation' or negative imagery of the father, especially if presented in a way that is threatening to the mother-child bond. Needless to say, indirect contact with a child is the same as no contact at all, (especially below a child's late-teens), given the need of a child to have a physical presence and their inability to intellectualise relationships in the same way an adult.

In conclusion, a father who has an ex who wants to eradicate him from her child(ren)'s lives, and is not merely in a high conflict separation, has to act quickly. The longer he delays making decisions the sooner irreversible choices are made for him.

Changing country

If you decided to permanently move your child abroad, (over whom you have PR), from his or her usual place of residence, but without the permission of all those who have PR for that child, you can never safely return to this country. However, it matters when and how you do this for there are grades of lawlessness. Although what will not change, whichever way you do things, is the damage to the child and the childless-parent left behind.

Nevertheless, some fathers decide that what is best is to remove their children to a saner jurisdiction. France, for example, faced with an intractable dispute between parents over child arrangements has been known to order children to be taken into care until the parents do co-operate. In this way, neither parent wins (something that to me sounds sensible).

Taking your children, or causing them to be sent, out of the United Kingdom for more than one month (28 days) without the permission of all the parties listed in the 1984 Child Abduction Act (CAA 1984) Sections 1 and 6, (e.g. a mother and father with PR both have to agree) is potentially an offence under that Act, punishable by a maximum of **7 years in prison** for each child taken e.g. 14 years for two children. This punishment applies to any parent and any person who assists in the sending or taking. Also, the same punishment is executable for detaining a child abroad for more than 28 days, once sent, if not with the permission of all those mentioned in CAA 1984. However, it is not illegal for a child to be taken to Scotland. If that can be proven to be the jurisdiction of the child at the time of removal from the UK then Scottish laws apply, and the punishment is then a maximum of two years in prison.

There are legal defences that can be used under the CAA 1984. These are if the abducting parent: thought they had the permission of the other relevant person(s), could not contact the other person(s) or that the other person(s) were unreasonable in their refusal to allow the removal. Such abductions can, therefore, be less serious than at first may be thought, especially if the losing parent is slow to complain, if the child's residence has been shared between several countries or the complaining person was involved in the transfer of the child. While defences may be arguable if the relevant person is just the other parent, when a Family Court Order is made under CA 1989 the whole thing becomes more black and white and far more serious for an abductor. All children subject to Family Court Orders require the permission of a Family Court for removal, by either parent or anyone else with PR. An abductor under these circumstances will have not only committed an offence under the CAA 1984, but will also be in contempt of court, (a criminal act).

Once removed, a child can potentially be forcibly returned to their last place of residence using the Hague Convention of 1980 if the originating country is a signatory to that Convention. However, such an application must be made within one year of a claimed abduction. The Law Act used in the UK to evoke this Convention is the Child Abduction and Custody Act 1985. Legal defence of applications for the return of a child can include: that the parent wanting the return was not exercising custody at the time of removal, that to return a child to their original place of residence would place them in danger of abuse, or that it is in contravention of a child's human rights or contrary to the wishes of a Gillick Competent child (one judged competent to know their mind as though an adult).

Once abduction has happened effectively two things begin: 1) a race by the parent who has abducted his child(ren) to establish residence in the new country, and 2) a race for the parent from whom the children have been abducted to find and locate them and to bring an action under the Hague Convention. At the same time, the abducting parent will have to face the consequences of breaching CAA 1984, (although breaking of this law is unlikely to become an Interpol Red Listed event).

It cannot be overemphasised the strength of venom that comes from the UK's Judiciary over child abduction by angry fathers – see the dedication at the start of this book. There is a strong inclination in the CPS (Crown Prosecution Service) to have such fathers charged with kidnapping and abduction, and this former crime carries **life in prison** as a punishment. If you do not have PR as a father, and you abduct your child, this is almost certainly with what you will be charged.

In short, fathers who buck the system of the Family Courts are persecuted as pillared examples to us all. One of the reasons for this ferociousness is that abduction does work. A 2011 report in *The Telegraph* estimated that there are 500 cases per year. Often such acts only fail because of a 'Ronnie Biggs Syndrome' (of the Great Train Robbery fame), where a father returns to the UK once his children have grown up, thinking things will be forgotten (and they never are).

Changing residence

Getting a court to drop a No Contact Order is like the search for the Philosopher's Stone. Many dream of and struggle to attain such a thing, and some say a way does exist, and will even quote cases. However, in all the recounting I have heard, — for I have never seen it myself — there is always a twist. Either the No Contact Order did not in truth exist, but was an interim order or something else, or the opposing party made some humongous legal gaff.

While it is no use to a father who already has a No Contact Order, my main advice is that if there is one sure way of beating the Family Courts it is reversing the residence of your children **before a court case starts**. For if you can somehow, without using abduction, legally change your status to that of a sole-resident parent, (even though this term is officially done away with in legislation), the courts can — but do not always — start backing you as the sole-parent (even if you are a man).

There are soft ways I have known of this being achieved. In one instance, the children of a separated-couple ended up living with their father in Denmark, after their mother returned to the UK. She applied to have her kids join her, but this was denied in the Danish equivalent of Family Courts. So she pretended to have reconciliation with the father and even returned to his bed. Using her womanly wiles, she convinced him that all that was wrong in their relationship was living away from her home country. Persuaded in this way the father re-joined his wife in the UK, bringing both their children with him. One day he came back home from work and... but I bet you've guessed. After locking out her ex-husband, she got full custody of her children in the subsequent UK Family Court case, and the father never saw them again. Amazing what changing the locks and a feminist-dictated police force can do to a man, isn't it?

I have heard of, but not assisted in, similar case with the genders reversed. For instance, I am told that a father (helped by a Father's Support Group) had been physically thrown out of his home by his partner's brother. He then applied and got social housing, claiming he was a victim of domestic abuse. His ex then made the unbelievable mistake of asking the father for help with his children, for a couple of days. He agreed, but then immediately got an emergency injunction to keep her from contacting their children, or going near him, using CDA to get Legal Aid funding of the whole application. The mother was then in an extremely weak position to get any contact with her children via the courts.

In this last scenario, it should be noted that the father was not working so it was self-evident to a court that he could act in a mother's role. Secondly, his partner made a daft mistake. Unfortunately, most mothers truly determined to remove a father from their children's lives do not make mistakes.

Another way, — a way most fathers reach for in an almost knee-jerk reaction to being denied contact — is to invoke the mysterious powers of social workers to do the job of switching child-residence for you. Such action can only be invoked by claiming abuse of children by the parent who is exercising sole-residency. I have had three parent-clients who have had this done to them, two men and one woman. In each situation I was left dumbfounded.

It seems that some Local Authority Children Services staff employ a tactic of piggybacking off police powers, under Section 46 of the CA 1989, (although it is not ever stated as such). For sure, social workers have no powers of entry into a person's private house without Court Orders, and the social workers in my clients' cases had no such orders. However, in each situation the 'accused resident-parent' was enticed into a meeting, and in that was met by the police and the social worker. In the next instant their child, or children, were marched out of sight and re-housed with the other, estranged parent, who also had PR. The social worker and the police then stepped back with no further meetings, no case reviews, and no Court Orders. The childless-parent was then left to finance a Private Family Law application to try and get their children back.

I was asked how social services can abduct children in this way, without Court Orders, over accusations that, in all three cases, were minor in the extreme, not proven in any court, and over which the police were taking no action at all. I have to admit there are ways of working between the police and social services which have become unfathomable to the average person. These are mixed-up in amendments to the CA 1989, such as the Children Act 2004.

I would caution a father from holding out hope of residence being switched in this way; something that will not happen if a No Contact Order is in existence. Generally, the mostly mono-gender institution of social services is very sensitive to men trying to muckrake against mothers. Allegations made by fathers, even really severe ones, even ones with concrete evidence, will fall on deaf ears if the consensus in a Local Authority bureaucracy is against them. Finally, even if a father does nevertheless achieve a switch of sole-residence, he is then faced with a bitter task: to do to the mother what she would do to him, for he cannot then afford to give the mother a chance to undo his achievement by allowing his children any contact with her. Needless to say, having a father as the only biological parent harms children just as much as having only a biological mother.

AN OPEN PLEA

Family Courts do not have the ability to fairly look inside an unmonitored marriage or cohabitation and settle personal arguments about the faults and allegations parents may ascribe to each other as they go through a separation. For this reason, if judicial intervention is sought, it can only rightly take limited action. If this interference becomes corrupted to the point a court feels compelled to take sides on an inhumane proposition, e.g. to take children away from one parent on the say-so of the other, the whole thing becomes an evil abomination.

In those very rare cases that a father does commit a crime of physically or sexually abusing his children, that is something entirely different. Yet, laws already exist to allow criminal convictions to be taken into account in the Family Courts, and such convictions could lead to an order of limited supervised or no contact. It is, therefore, wholly inexcusable to allow the inadequate Family Court processes to circumnavigate a father's right to be heard in a robust Criminal Court, with a jury, on matters of such extreme importance as to whether he is guilty of being abusive in his own home or should be allowed to bring up his children. This is something more important than life, death, or money and deserves the full resources of the courts in its treatment.

I struggle for words to express the strength of my feelings about those who make No Contact Orders against fathers under Private Family Law alone. Family Courts were not set up to do this, but have evolved into it. My spiritual side holds tight, with fingers white from the strain, to the precept that there are no bad people, only bad acts. Yet, what Judges and social workers do then when they use Private Law to take children from loving fathers is as bad as bad gets. It can never be justified.

Works cited, but not referenced in the text

21. **Bauer, Patricia J; Larkina, Marina.** *The onset of childhood amnesia in childhood: A prospective investigation of the course and determinants of forgetting of early-life events.* [Memory. (22nd November, 2014) (8): 907–924].

16

What is the Way Forward?

"Each time a man stands up for an ideal, or acts to improve the lot of others, or strikes out against injustice, he sends forth a tiny ripple of hope…" Senator Kennedy, Robert F. [Quote from a speech at the University of Cape Town, South Africa; 1966].

THE POSITIVES

Some report that the behaviour of Family Courts over child arrangements has abated from its extremes seen at the turn of the 21st Century in the UK. One FNF branch organiser commented that decisions are now, "Not that bad."

The reign of Bulter-Sloss, Hale and Potter, all nutcase feminists to some degree or another, have thankfully past. What has replaced them seem to be a series of vanilla Heads of Division, with no hidden gender-agenda, not changing things too much save making the job of the Family Courts more manageable. While bias legislation continues to be poured onto the statute books (through the mechanisms identified earlier), one of the main instruments of Family Court discrimination has been removed, at least for now, namely: a feminist Head of the Family Court Division.

The trend for Child Arrangement Cases to be brought by Litigants in Person in the Family Courts, aided by changes to forms and processes, and the accompanied removal of Legal Aid for all but those willing to claim domestic abuse, on the whole, is a positive. Separation without a lawyer now accounts for three-quarters of **all** family break-ups in the UK – self-arranged and via the Family Courts. While Legal Aid for false accusers is still a great source of injustice, kicking out lawyers in family break-ups is for the greater good. Lawyers are massively overpaid for what they do, and while their removal may not alter injustice in the Family Courts, which still goes on, it helps to get these injustices done without the added insult of life-changing amounts of wasted time and money.

Finally, there are signs that biases put in place for the express purpose of giving women an unfair advantage in child-arrangement disputes are now tripping over themselves. Such prejudices tended to be attached to things women traditionally had, such as the residence of children at the outset of a court case. However, in those cases where this is not so, courts now act against an absent mother as though she were a man. For example, women who walk away from a family of children for a career move, a new lover, temporary dislike of their children, or economic gain, despite trying all the usual tricks of false allegations and so on, find they cannot whatever they do get residence back.

I believe it was not like this before as a workingman taking on a mother's role was in the past not seen as tenable, as it is now.

THINGS THAT HAVE GOT WORSE

All that separated fathers ask of the Family Courts, who settle 50 per cent of all family break-ups in the UK, is to live with their children for a greater amount of their non-school time than a mother wants to give. Something as simple as a repeal of Section 1 (2B) of the 1989 Children Act would be enough, ending the idea that indirect contact in any way goes towards involvement with both parents. A change in line with the new Australian and or existing USA Family Laws, that shared-residence as a presumption is better for a child than residence with only one prime parent, would be an enlightened step forward for our country.

In July 2010, Brian Binley MP introduced a Private Member's Bill, the *Shared Parenting Orders Bill*, which aimed to create a legal presumption that shared-parenting orders should be the default arrangement in Private Family Law Child Arrangement Orders. At the end of March 2011, Charlie Elphick MP introduced a second Private Members' Bill, the *Children's Access to Parents Bill* which had comparable objectives. In 2011, a Ministerial Task Force on Childhood and the Family started to look at the same issue and was made-up of the highest elected officials in the country in a gender-balanced team of three women and three men: Prime Minister, David Cameron; Deputy Prime Minister, Theresa May; Secretary of State for Work and Pensions, Duncan Smith; Minister of State for the Department of Education, Sarah Teather; Economics Secretary to the Treasury, Justine Greening and Under-Secretary of State for Health, Anne Milton. At the same time a Family Justice Review Committee, Headed by David Norgrove, looked at the Family Courts with shared-parenting orders on its agenda. Norgrove's 2011 report fed into a Parliamentary Bill Review Committee, which had 21 members: 10 women and 11 men.

Things were looking up for the millions of UK fathers estranged from their children.

Yet, despite all of this attention and an even split of decision makers between the genders, the result was the Children and Family Act 2014 (CFA 2014), which for fathers seeking Section 8 Orders is a total disaster. CFA 2014 not only failed to include any clause for a presumption of shared-residency, it also failed to remove that key clause of the CA 1989: Section 1 (2B). Yet worse, it tried to remove a central piece of armoury a father has in a case where CAFCASS are against him, namely an expert witness that can properly report the thoughts and wishes of his children as well as comment on the effect of parent alienation by a mother. For the CFA 2014 explicitly attacks the use of expert witnesses to assess children at the request of a father.

How society missed an opportunity for a reform of Family Law speaks to how the situation in the Family Courts came into being. For in the Norgrove Committee, as well as the Parliamentary Bill Review Committee, information supporting a mothers' view came from well-resourced woman support institutions. In contrast, evidence examined by the committees for a fathers' viewpoint relied on amateurs with no funding at all. What is more, men in the committees were not united in their views, whereas the women were.

It is a common situation. Men as a gender, unlike women, do not naturally unite together unless they are part of a regimented organisation – in which case they are unstoppable and the makers of worlds. Besides, it is generally the case that the plight of any man, even a father, does not draw empathy in the way of a child or woman. So, unless the men on the committees had personal experience of losing their children through the Family Courts they would be unlikely to have any idea what all the fuss was about – and needless to say none had gone through the courts.

As if the above was not enough, the Norgrove Committee then used bloody great nails to bolt in place the gynocentric position, by laying down rules (in an interim report) before any committee member had a chance to start work. These rules were:

"No legislation should be introduced that creates or risks creating the perception that there is an assumed parental right to substantial shared or equal time for both parents."

In other words, the debate was closed before it had started.

How did this happen? We cannot know the exact political machinations (apart from anything else Brian Binley is no longer an MP, and he has refused to comment). Yet, if you look, the evidence used in making the interim report was limited to Helen Rhoades of the University of Melbourne, and she held that changes in the law in Australia towards shared-parenting had been a failure. What is more, the Norgrove interim report presented a fait accompli for later discussion, based on the outcome of a late-day commons debate of the Children and Adoption Act, mostly attended by women MPs, in 2006. In this debate legislation for shared-parenting was deemed illegal, as it was inconsistent with the Paramountcy Principle of Family Law, (as the rights of any parent can never outweigh the needs of the child) and this precedent was carried over in the interim report.

Despite the strategies of anti-reformists some debate on shared-parenting did happen, albeit in a rearguard action. Professor P. Parkinson of the Centre for Separated Parents at the University of Sydney voiced a rebuttal of the opinions of Helen Rhoades; that in fact, families benefit from the changes of the law in Australia made in 2006, which were a success. There followed an official-looking review, not containing any new research, by a Belinda Fehlberg of the University of Oxford's Department of Social Policy and Intervention, who authored a report entitled: *Caring for children after parental separation: would legislation for shared parenting time help children?* Not surprisingly, Belinda answered her question on behalf of her sister-parents and said: no. A small team of amateurs calling themselves the Men's Aid Charity desperately tried to point out the falsehoods in Ms Fehlberg's report, in a self-financed response which in fairness was also entered into the Bill Review Committee as evidence. Yet, mostly this group tripped over their lack of resources.

There were many other perversions of the evidence presented to the committees examining shared-parenting, including from the public consultation, to which I contributed. I am sure the majority-female Civil Service did dutifully collect all comments from both women and men. However, the key thing omitted was that the vast majority of responses were from men, and they all said the same thing. Instead, only one such comment on each view was used.

In the final analysis, before anything was on the table of a Bill Review Committee, the die had already been cast. The divided-male camp and the united sisterhood for gynocentric laws saw the private members' bills dashed on the rocks of politics. As a result, fathers of Great Britain today remain second-class parents.

Some of the key points used in the decision to maintain the status quo are publicly available in the papers used by the committees. These arguments clearly show how political manoeuvring had debunked all semblances of rational thought. The published reasons for the decisions were:

1). Following divorce or separation 90 per cent of families settle things between themselves. Any change to legislation in the Family Courts would therefore only benefit a minority, as the majority of families make arrangements outside of the courts.

2). In a connected point, it follows that those families which do go to court over child arrangement disputes are 'high conflict', and often the father has been abusive or the parents are so opposed to each other that they are incapable of bringing up their children together.

3). It, therefore, follows that the welfare of children will necessarily be in conflict with any new law that gives a parent an assumed right to have substantial parenting-time with their children following separation or divorce. For example, a presumption of shared-parenting would give fathers the right to continue their abuse of a mother and/or children, and/or would perpetuate family dysfunction.

4). Shared parenting is detrimental to a child as they need a single, stable home and cannot cope with having two homes, even when each home contains a natural parent to that child.

5). Families, who have or have not been to court, rarely exercise 50:50 shared parenting as it is so impractical. About 50 per cent of families surveyed in a study have a contact parent who rarely sees their children, and 50 per cent have a 70:30 or 60:40 arrangement of overnight stays. Families in court cases wanting 50:50 shared parenting are therefore actually pursuing personal rights over children's needs.

6). As the quality of parenting-time is more important than the amount of time spent with a child, children will not suffer in those cases where a court orders children spend little time with their father, if they have a caring-father.

7). Uncaring or abusive fathers are unable to render quality parenting-time. So, as long as a court does not give them many opportunities to manipulate family members, children of such fathers will eventually cut them out of their own accord and so be better off.

It should be self-evident to anyone why these arguments are false and misandrist in their intent, but if not, let me give you a few pointers:

i). In reply to the first argument, there are 12-million heterosexual married-couples in the UK, and 40 per cent of these have dependent children. We also know that there are 102,000 divorces per year, a rate of about 0.8 per cent per year of the installed-base of heterosexual married-people. This figure needs to be compared with the annual number of Child Arrangement court cases of 51,000 per year. In other words, you could speculate that half of all divorces end up in court looking for a Child Arrangement Order. You might contest that some of these divorces do not involve dependent children. So, if we suppose that divorces are spread evenly across families with, and families without dependent children, then simple extrapolation would imply 40,000 of divorces in the UK per year involve dependent children. If we add in cohabiting-couples with dependent children (which ONS figures put at one million) and assume these divorce at the same rate as married couples, which again is a sharp downgrading of the likely figure, this gives us a UK total of 48,000 divorces with dependent children per year. In this analysis, **all** divorces or separations with children end up in the Family Courts.

There clearly are other factors, such as some Family Court cases involving repeat visits by couples already divorced and so on. Yet, given what we know, the members of the Family Law Review were either lying or deceived when they claimed 90 per cent of people make their own child arrangements after divorce or separation. A lot of questioning after the event found that the false figure of 90 per cent had simply been a rumour, circulated between girlfriends in the Civil Service, which members of the committees took as fact. In other words it was gossip.

ii). In the connected point, (point 2), people know what sort of orders come out of Family Courts, for despite laws on confidentiality people talk and things get spread around.

What people do in private settlements, therefore, reflects court policy. If Family Courts always side with one party over another, fathers who do not go to court will be far more likely to give in to whatever a mother wants by way of contact with his children. In this way, the prejudice of the Family Courts affects the whole of our society, not just those who go to court. Proof of this is found in the number of families with children, and no biological fathers, which has increased to one-third of all families, with one million UK children now having no substantial contact with their real fathers.

The ugly truth is that the Family Courts create high conflict in family break-ups, and this would not be so if it were known that the Family Courts were fair.

iii). Far from following on, points one and two above have no logical connection to an axiom that shared-parenting contradicts the Paramountcy Principle of Family Law. For underlying such a proposition is the concept that abuse of children and women underpins all family break-ups, which is misandrist disinformation. In reality, it is the arrogance and selfishness of a parent in dismissing the importance of the other parent which underpins most applications for removing a parent from children's lives. An assumption of shared-parenting would **instil** the Paramountcy Principle in Family Law by forcing an applicant seeking to remove the other parent from a family to prove this need beyond all reasonable doubt, and preferably in a Criminal Court.

iv). Contending, without proof, that children cannot cope with two homes has always been absurd. It is a proposition that implies residential schools are an abuse of children, and that the nations of the USA and Australia (that both have instigated a presumption of shared-parenting) harm children. Objective social science from America is clear: **not** having shared-parenting after a family separation can result in significant harm, or risk of harm, to children.

v). Shared-parenting is defined as both parents having a child live with them for no less than one-third of the child's out-of-school hours. The study quoted, therefore, confirms, rather than denies, that in 50 per cent of cases of self-arranged separations in the UK, not involving the courts, shared-parenting was implemented.

vi). Replacing adequate time with a mythical 'quality-parenting-time' denies all science on what it takes to be a parent. It is a contemptible feminist proposition that seeks to cruelly justify a policy of denying a father the time he needs to bring up his children effectively.

vii). In point 7, the committee once again relies on a thesis domestic abuse is the reason for all family break-ups. Whereas the real reason the amount of time a father spends with his children is ever disputed is because mothers know such separation will de-bond their children from their father, and this is something they want. Denying a father the right to live with their children for sufficient time is inhuman, an abuse and a denial of a person's human rights when the decision is made without a fair trial, or jury. Such parental abuse is the concern of the Family Courts, despite their denial, as it connects with the abuse of children.

What this brief analysis of one of the many attempts to change legislation shows is that this State still has corrupt niches of feminism in its Central Government Civil Service. These are being allowed to run gender-agendas to shape discriminatory 'Hale-type' statutes against fathers. It is probably more rampant now than it has ever been. Meanwhile, the bias in CAFCASS and Local Authorities continues to be as vast and unapologetic as is the clear dominance of a single-gender in nearly all of their job roles. At the same time, the fraud of domestic abuse being widespread in UK families continues to drive a colossal Government over-funding of anti-share-parenting extremists in both mother and now father-assessment organisations, (such as the Respect Project). Even as I write £75 million has been allocated for domestic abuse relief during the Coronavirus outbreak, but not one penny for fathers denied all contact with their children by mothers using social isolation as an excuse to break visitation orders. These feminists are brazen in their influence over the Civil Service, even within the Department of Justice and the BBC.

The mechanisms used by the feminist lobby remind me of how a small group of Protestant fanatics managed to usher in America's era of prohibition, something only a tiny minority of people wanted. For the Prohibition legislation (or Volstead Act) piggybacked a law everyone did want, driven by a hatred of Germans and the need to feed overseas American soldiers during WWI. As a result, grain that would have been used for beer production (by German breweries) was redirected to the war effort by banning the manufacture of beer. A small but powerful lobby of Protestants then seized the bureaucratic-momentum to extend this Law Act to include the banning of all alcohol. Similarly, today the public's distaste of the idea of abuse of women and children is being exploited in the UK by a tiny elite of well-connected and financed feminists, to introduce misandrist legislation that people in general do not want. This lawmaking is now set to go beyond the Family Courts under the heading of a Domestic Abuse Act. Even as I write, feminist control of our language is about to be enshrined in statutes which threaten to reclassify the expression of anti-feminist thoughts, (such as printed here), a 'hate crime' punishable with imprisonment.

HOW DO WE GET OUT OF THIS?

If I could wave a magic wand I would close the Family Courts for Private Law Children Act cases, cancel the entire Children Act 1989, (and all its amendments), and disband CAFCASS. I would replace the lot with a simple tribunal whose sole purpose would be to arbitrate on the suitability of shared-parenting arrangements following divorce or separation, (in a world where property settlements were a clear 50:50). Any transgression from the determination of this tribunal would be sanctioned with the residence of children going to the sole care of the parent denied contact. Then I would invent the male pill, one that did not damage male libido or fertility, so that women could no longer get pregnant without the express permission of their partner – so eliminating the majority of children born to families destined for separation. Yet, none of this is going to happen, now is it?

Many people in Father Support Groups despair at what seems to them a tsunami of hate against men, especially against separated-fathers who are **all** portrayed as woman abusers. Feminism seems to be the root cause and the reason why the public at large are so uncaring of the abominable injustices that come from the UK's Family Courts. For many, things seem to have gone so far wrong that nothing can get us out of this mess.

I disagree.

Female control of societies is as old as time. It emerges in history as far back as Cleopatra's or Boadicea's time. As a past student of Experimental Psychology, I draw analogies to our ape cousins and how, under the right conditions, females largely control the running of their societies, (albeit with a few dominant males at their head). There is nothing new in what we are going through. Admittedly, in human history, women's control of civilisation is usually followed by the complete collapse of a nation – but it is not new.

Feminism, in various guises, has been around since its inception by a man, Friedrich Engels, in the 1840s. It has come and gone a few times, claiming credit for things that were happening anyway. Suffragettes, for instance, while nowadays a term widely considered as synonymous with women's liberation, were a predominantly male movement, fighting for British citizens' universal right to vote in political elections. These activists, who had both male and women branches, threatened revolution unless the vote was changed from being the sole preserve of the property-owning classes, and given to the masses, (and in 1780 less than 250,000 of the entire population of Great Britain had the right to vote).

Suffrage movements won the right to vote for British people of both sexes, regardless of their ownership of property or how much they paid in rent (as before), in a series of stages, implemented in iterations of the Representation of the People Act. The culmination of the Suffragette's work was in 1918 when for the first time all men over 21 years old, and all women over 30 years old, were given the vote (as an appeasement to the masses for their efforts in the Great War). This left women between the ages of 21 and 30 years without a political franchise, for the next ten years (until these too were given the vote in 1928). Feminist rewrites of history may latterly claim that the Women's Branch of Suffragettes were solely responsible for getting the vote for all women, but in fact, the job was done by men – and the vote would have been given to younger women in the same time had Emmeline Pankhurst not existed at all. Similarly, most of what we now credit in the Family Courts as the work of feminists is the unintended consequences of actions by men, for the betterment of British society, in the period 1950–60 (see chapter nine).

Society in England may now be subjected to feminist-ideology in some corners of British legislation, but in general there is no deep-seated support for battle-of-the-sexes feminism – and there never will be. Most know that men cherish, love and want to protect women and not to do them harm. Sure, this may be driven by a powerful and base-animal instinct to mate, but these sentiments are nonetheless real. It is also self-evident that men and women are designed, as sexual animals, to be at odds with each other, in many ways. Tension between the sexes is part of the human condition, and to deny it as normal is to deny being human.

What perhaps has led to the apparent four decades of feminist influence in the Family Courts is environmental change. Not only the change in the State's support for lone-mother families, but changes in the total population of Great Britain – that in my lifetime has nearly doubled. Perhaps, as a result, our population also has an unhealthy profile; with a majority of citizens economically inactive, retired and owning nearly all of the country's vital assets, i.e. homes. As a result, overpriced housing has for some time now impoverished UK families-with-dependent-children, (largely due to idiosyncratic building restrictions and a refusal to provide social housing or rent controls – as found in the rest of Europe).

In ape troops there are allegories. When these social animals experience overcrowding they react with a decline of breeding in the young, which is done later in life and with far less success, not least because of social pressures from old matriarchs who rule the roost and may even oust breeding males. Sound familiar?

How we British live our family lives will undoubtedly, over time, swing back to a more natural interdependency of parental roles. Perhaps the demographics in Great Britain first need to shift again. Yet, in the meantime, an evil state of affairs exists. For this reason, we need to give the pendulum of time a shove. What is needed is a shock to the system to bring this country's treatment of family separations back into the realms of common sense and civilised morality.

In 2017 a fledgeling organisation started, The Doubtfire Fund, whose role was to find a crack in the bias of Family Courts into which a wedge of change could be driven. The crack found was: No Contact Orders; and the wedge: Group Litigation in the European Courts of Human Rights.

Shortly after the end of WWII, the UK bound itself to a European Convention on Human Rights (ECHR). At the highest levels this country agreed to follow the rulings of courts that adjudicate on this Convention – and this has nothing to do with the EU (European Union), which is something that came much later. The ECHR did not change the law of a signatory country unless the Human Rights Convention is enacted within that country, which in the UK it has not. However, the commitment to the Convention of Human Rights binds the UK State to follow the recommendations on cases ECHR Courts examine, and to award compensation if so found to be owed.

Fathers, and other non-resident parents, have been unhappy with orders from the UK's Family Courts since gender-prejudice within them became rampant in the 1990s. Given the Ministry of Justice's estimate of the number of Child Arrangement cases handled per year, to be an average of 50,000 (1), this equates to 1.5 million families who have potentially been wronged. Within this population there is a special group, estimated to be about 220,000 strong: those that received 'No Contact Orders' from the Family Courts, and who had no Criminal or Public Law case levied against them to support such an order.

These No Contact Orders are wrong under the ECHR, according to Articles 6–8: The Right to a Fair Trial, No Punishment without Law, and the Right to respect for Private and Family Life. For example, just dealing with Article 6, because no contact is such a severe order it is arguable that the UK has a duty of care to ensure such decisions are the product of a scrupulously-fair trial process, similar to that found in Criminal Courts. Yet, as has been discussed, in the UK Family Courts there is no use of juries, no requirement for both parties to be equally legally represented, no requirement to disclose or have any evidence, and there is no requirement for a Judge to ensure contentions are proved beyond reasonable doubt.

I would contend that the UK is special in the use of Family Law courts. While many Family courts around the world suffer the fault of being too lenient with mothers, few go as far as the UK in removing all contact of a child with their father, without a Criminal or Public Law trial, but on the say-so of a mother alone. No other State also has such duplicitous Family Laws as the UK, that claim 'no direct contact' means involvement of both parents with their child(ren). For all the above, and many other reasons, I would suggest that **all** UK fathers wronged by Family Court No Contact Orders are contenders for claiming compensation through the ECHR.

The action that could be employed to make this claim is called 'Group Litigation', what in America is referred to as a Class Action. Further, there is a mechanism within International Law for calculating compensation in this situation, within Case Law of fathers who sued a Nation-State for being unjustly separated from their children, e.g. involving asylum seekers. In these cases fathers were awarded around US $10,000 per month of wrongful separation, per child.

The Doubtfire Fund proposed bringing a Group Litigation claim, on behalf of fathers who have suffered No Contact Orders in the UK, to a European-based ECHR Court, (for the UK has such a court but it also has powers to ignore the convention when this conflicts with National Law). The Respondent in this claim would be the Nation-State of the UK, (not the Judiciary, Civil Service or Government, all of which would turn a civil claim into a Judicial Review). If successful this has the potential to generate substantial compensation as restitution for the UK allowing the kidnap of children from innocent, loving fathers. In addition, it would penalise the country in a way that could not be ignored, so that changes would have to follow or the UK would evermore face international derision as well as further claims.

While it existed, the Doubtfire Fund tried to raise funds to run a phased rollout of the above litigation. In overview the steps were: 1 a legal opinion on the feasibility of different types of action, followed by; 2 a case-collection phase and finishing with; 3 a court application, partly financed via a commission-taking law firm.

One way out of this mess is, therefore, for someone to fund the initial phase of the above Group Litigation on behalf of all UK fathers historically given No Contact Orders.

There are other suggestions.

While Judicial Reviews have been attempted by several Fathers' Rights pressure groups they have always concentrated on individual court cases. What has not been tried is a Judicial Review, (as opposed to a Select Committee Investigation), of the way some of the more anti-male legislation came into being with regards to the affiliation of key players to gender-bias organisations, (either directly, or via personal connections). For while the UK may have a climate in which extremist views can flourish only a few have exploited this mood, and are behind most of the misandrist Family Court Practice Directions and Law Acts that have left so many of the UK's children in a mess. A Judicial Review could, therefore, root out these influencers and cast doubt on the veracity of the legislation they helped bring onto the Statute Books.

Finally, over the years there are literally hundreds of thousands of instances of Family Law Fact-Finding Hearings that have found false allegations as true. Each instance has led to life-changing orders which were wrong and destructive to family lives. While the children subject to these orders may or may not have suffered, fathers certainly have.

Under Family Law the consequences of a wrong court decision on a father's wellbeing has no recourse. Yet in other branches of Civil Law being denied your right to bring up your children because of the illegal action of another is something over which you could successfully sue. A lie in any court is perjury, and remains so even if someone initially gets away with it. If harmed by such lies a father may later claim compensation from the offender, and even seek a private criminal prosecution against them. If we also apply the principles of the #MeToo virtual campaign, then it should not matter how long ago this perjury was committed. Any father who has the money and the stomach for it could, and should, take those who kidnapped their children back into a Civil Court, if perjury was used (and if they've kept all the Family Court case bundles). It won't make things right with their kids, but it could help stem the tide of injustice for fathers.

Whether through a Group Action, a Judicial Review, or any other initiative, the mother-centric child-arrangement policy of UK Family Courts must be consigned to history, alongside other atrocities such as the racial segregation of Aboriginal children from their parents in Colonial Australia. Just like the UK's current attitude to shared-parenting, this was a result of Judges adopting a culturally-corrupted version of the Paramountcy Principle for the supposed 'best interests of the child'. In the future, British children should have the right to an upbringing shared between their biological parents, regardless of how many homes or other people this parenting involves. Two-home families should be seen as lifestyle choices rather than, as now, failures to be dealt with in kangaroo courts.

Works cited, but not referenced in the text

1. *Family Court Statistics Quarterly, England and Wales, Annual 2017 including October to December 2017,* [29th March, 2018].

References Listed by Number

1. *Family Court Statistics Quarterly, England and Wales, Annual 2017 October to December.* [S.l. Ministry of Justice, (29th March, 2018)].

2. **Huxley, Aldous.** *Brave New World.* S.l. Random House, 1932.

3. **Reed, Carol.** *Oliver!* Columbia Pictures, 1968.

4. **Hamlyn, Becky; Coleman, Emma; Sefton, Mark.** *Mediation Information and Assessment Meetings and Mediation in private family law disputes. Quantitative research findings.* S.l. : Ministry of Justice Analytical Series, 2015

5. **Munby, Sir James.** *Practice Guidance: Children Arbitration in the Family Court.* [(Online) Judiciary.gov website. 26th July, 2018].

6. **Coelho, Paulo.** *Manual of the Warrior of Light.* [S.l. Harper Colins, 2002].

7. *Trends in the solicitors' profession Annual Statistics Report 2017.* [The Law Society, June, 2018].

8. **Hilborne, Nick,** *Family Lawyers 'Disproportionately Female and White?'* [(Online), Legal Futures; Posted 2020].

9. **Trinder, Liz; Hunter, Rosemary; Hitchings, Emma; Miles, Joanna; Moorhead, Richard; Smith, Leanne; Sefton, Mark; Hinchly, Victoria; Bader, Kay; Pearce, Julia:** *Litigants in person in private family law cases.* [S.l. : Ministry of Justice, (2014)].

10. **Knipe, Emily.** *Families and Households: 2017.* [ONS, 8th November 2017].

11. **Elkin, Meghan.** *Domestic Abuse in England and Wales, in the year ending March 2018.* [ONS, 22nd November, 2018].

12. *Child Maltreatment 2015.* [U.S. Department of Health & Human Services].

13. *Analysis of Post LASPO Use of Non-Molestation Orders.* [FNF Analysis, 15th October, 2018].

14. *BBC Equality Information Report.* [2015/16].

15. **Collins, William.** [(Online) www.empathygap.uk. (2019)].

16. **Hicks, Joe; Allen, Grahame.** *A Century of Change.* [House of Commons Research Paper No. 99/11 (21st December, 1999)].

17. **Jaye, Cassie.** *The Red Pill* – video rushes from. [Interview with Erin Pizzey, published on YouTube (2016)].

18. *Lone parents with dependent children by marital status of parent, sex, UK 1996-2015.* [ONS April 2016, Ref: 005660].

19. *Lone Parent and Step families with dependent children and children eligible for child maintenance.* [ONS March 2016, Ref: 005452].
20. Institute for Government website report on gender balance in the Civil Service (1991-2019).
21. **Bauer, Patricia J; Larkina, Marina.** *The onset of childhood amnesia in childhood: A prospective investigation of the course and determinants of forgetting of early-life events.* [Memory. (22nd November, 2014) (8): 907–924].

Other references used within the text

Practice Guidance: McKenzie Friends (Civil and Family Courts). [Master of the Rolls, Ministry of Justice, (2010)].

Psychologists as expert witnesses in the Family Courts in England and Wales: Standards, competencies and expectations. [Family Justice Council and the British Psychological Society, (January, 2016)].
Solicitor's Guideline Hourly Rates. [2010, HM Courts and Tribunal Service].

Hadden, Jason M; Davies, Rhiannon. *How to Represent Yourself in the Family Court.* [2015, Little Brown Book Group].

Children Act 1989 Guidance and Regulations, Volume 1, Court Orders. [HM Stationery Office, 1991].

Francis, Connie. *Who's Sorry Now?* [MGM records, 1958].

The Legal Aid, Sentencing and Punishment of Offenders Act (LASPO) 2012 - Evidence Requirements for Private Family Law Matters.

Fabricius, W.V.; Braver, S.L.; Diaz, P. & Velez, C.E. (2010) *Custody and parenting time: Links to family relationships and wellbeing after divorce.* In **Lamb, M.** (Ed). *The father's role in child development,* [(5th Ed), pp201-260. Wiley & Sons: New Jersey].

Recent Trends in Divorce and Custody Litigation, [Academy Forum, Volume 29, Number 2, Summer, 1985].

Fehlberg, Belinda. *Caring for children after parental separation: would legislation for shared parenting time help children?*

Niebuhr, Reinhold. *The Serenity Prayer;* [1932-33].

Kennedy, Robert F. [Quote from a speech at the University of Cape Town, South Africa; 1966].

List of figures

APPENDIX I

Orders that can be made under Children Act 1989, Part I & II

These apply only to those who habitually living in England and Wales. To view the whole Law Act see **Appendix IV**

A Parental Responsibility Order – see Sections 2–4A, CA 1989. This order bestows PR on a biological father, or anyone else, if not obtained automatically through marriage, or removes PR from a father, (but not if PR was obtained through marriage). PR for a biological mother is automatic and cannot be removed under this sort of order.

A Child Arrangement Order – AKA a Section 8 Order. These may detail with whom a child shall reside and when, if a joint residence order, and when and where a person other than the person or people the child lives with will see a child in contact visits. The vast majority of Private Family Law cases ask for this type of order, often combined with other types.

A Specific Issue Order – AKA a Section 8 Order. This is an order on a specific important issue disputed between those who have parental responsibility for the same child. Examples might be: where a child is schooled or whether a child should be circumcised or not. This order can also compel a parent who had residence of a child to bring that child to the other parent to reside. The essential point is that it decides something a person with PR would normally be able to do by virtue of their PR, but is being prevented from doing by a dispute with someone else who has equal PR or guardianship rights over a child.

A Prohibitive Steps Order – AKA a Section 8 Order. This prevents a person from exercising their rights over a child they normally would have by virtue of their PR for that child. It is a sort of Injunction. An example would be: not to remove a child from a school or take them abroad. Often these orders are very cruel for fathers, such as saying they cannot try and make contact with their child by social media, phone or speak to them if they see them in the street.

Activity Directions/Conditions – see Section 11A–F. These are orders that can be attached to Child Arrangement Orders already in force, or can be standalone where a court is considering whether to make a Child Arrangement Order. They define an activity that **must** be carried out by a party to court proceedings, for example, as a condition for an existing Child Arrangement Order to continue or for a future order to be made. Activities that the Law Act specifically mentions include: programmes, classes and counselling sessions aimed at improving relationships with a child, (so this could be an order to attend sessions on how to reduce parent alienation or to address a person's violent behaviour). These conditions cannot include medical or psychiatric assessment or treatment, nor can they insist someone attends mediation. Activities cannot be imposed on a child, nor can they apply to anyone who lives outside of England and Wales, for example, in Scotland.

Enforcement Orders – Section 11J–L. An order made on application by one of the subjects of a Child Arrangements Order that requires another person, who has failed to comply with this same order, to do unpaid community work. The subject of an enforcement order must be over 18 years old and habitually reside in England or Wales. Before the order can be made an investigation is needed by a Cafcass worker, or the Welsh equivalent, and consideration is given to the impact on the child named in the Child Arrangements Order. These orders can be in addition to, or instead of, a Contempt of Court finding that may result in a jail term and/or a fine.

Compensation for Financial Loss Order – Section 11 O. Made in the case where a person's breach of a Child Arrangement Order has led to another person, also named on the order, making a financial loss. For example, if a parent refused to send a child for a pre-arranged holiday, which caused the other to lose the cost of the holiday.

Change of Name and/or Removal from Jurisdiction Orders – Section 13. Any child who is subject to a Child Arrangement Order cannot have their name changed, by anyone, or be removed from the United Kingdom for more than one month, without the permission of a Family Court. This order allows either or both of these things to be done.

Family Assistance Order – Section 16. An order that can last a maximum of 12 months, for a social worker to befriend and help maintain family relationships, but only between those mentioned in the order. For example, this could be between a mother and her child, to help the child overcome a desire to live with their father. It could also name both parents, but doesn't have to, if they are both named in a Child Arrangements Order. Such orders require the agreement of all those named in the order, except the child(ren), and the agreement of a named Local Authority. This order can also require a parent to keep a court informed of their address, and also require a social worker to report on the continued applicability of any Section 8 Orders.

Monitoring Order – Section 11G–H. There are two types of monitoring orders, as well as the one under the Family Assistance Order. This is where a social worker is ordered to check on any party to a Child Arrangements Order, other than a child, to see if they are complying with the details in that order. Or, an order for a social worker to check on an individual's compliance with an Activity Direction or a condition attached to a Child Arrangements Order.

9114 Order – see Section 91 (14). AKA a 'Baring Order'. These bar a person who has made several applications to the Family Court from making any more without first going through a screening process in a separate court hearing. Baring orders apply to a particular person making applications for any Private Family Law order, or for only some types of orders. For example, an applicant may have a Barring Order of making any more applications for Section 8 Orders, but not applications for enforcement of an existing Section 8 Order.

APPENDIX II – Useful Forms

Other forms, not mentioned elsewhere in this book, that you are likely to need or come-across as a litigant using Private Family Law and which concern a child arrangement, or a related order. NB: For information on how to get these forms see **Appendix IV.**

SOME ADDITIONAL FORMS USED IN LOWER COURT CHILD ARRANGEMENT CASES.

Form C1: Apply for certain orders under the Children Act 1989 – used as a catch all for orders that do not fall under other forms.

Form C2: Make an application in existing court proceedings relating to children – frequently reached for by fathers frustrated by the length of court proceedings and wanting some interim order to change the arrangements for contact with his children while a court case continues. They are also used to apply for things missed out in Interim Hearings, e.g. when a party suddenly realises he needs extra evidences, such as an expert report to bolster their case. This form is also used to apply for permission to apply for a C100 order if you are subject to a 9114 Order.

Form C4: Ask the court to order someone to give information about where a child is – particularly used when a no contact order is given and the mother moves house so that a father cannot even write to his child(ren).

Form C8: Apply to keep your contact details confidential from other parties in family proceedings – used mostly in cases of parties claiming they are subject to domestic abuse, although the ease of obtaining Injunctions in Family Courts reduces the need for these sorts of applications. In fact fathers seem to use these more than mothers.

Form C79: Apply to the court to enforce a child arrangements order. Used to apply for enforce of a Child Arrangement Process Order of a Family Court, which has been broken by one of the parties to that order.

Form C78: Application for attachment of a Warning Notice to a child arrangements order. Little needed nowadays as most orders of Family Court do carry a Warning Notice, (as standard wording at the end of an order) but can be something needed if an order was made via a self-devised out-of-court agreement, ratified by a Judge, particularly if the parties had no legal representation. The warning notice is a necessary inclusion if a sanction, a punishment, is to be applied for not obeying the order.

Form C66: Application for an order under the High Court inherent jurisdiction in relation to children. This is effectively applying for a ruling to be made concerning a particular situation that is not covered by existing laws, or is so complex the matter cannot be dealt with by the Lower Courts.

FORMS FOR GETTING PR WHEN THERE IS NO DISPUTE BETWEEN PARENTS.

A series of forms exist that allow someone to acquire Parental Responsibility over a child that they did not get automatically. These are used in an uncontested, mutual consent agreement. These forms can be filled in and stamped at a Magistrate's Court without the need for a hearing:

Form C (PRA1): Ask the court to witness your Parental Responsibility agreement.
Form C (PRA2): Ask the court to witness your step-parent Parental Responsibility agreement.
Form C (PRA3): Parental Responsibility Agreement. Section 4ZA Children Act 1989 (acquisition of Parental Responsibility by second female parent).

FORMS FOR INTERNATIONAL CHILD ARRANGEMENT DISPUTES

Form C68: Application for international transfer of jurisdiction to or from England and Wales. For a child custody matter previously decided in another country, or started to be decided in a court case in another country, which is moved to the UK, or moves from the UK to another country, then this form is part of a series of formalities to transfer the court rulings and further hearings to or from the UK. There is a whole bunch of other forms you can use for international child custody disputes:

Form C62: Certificate referred to in Article 42(1) of Council Regulation (EC) No. 2201/2003 of 27 November 2003(1) concerning the return of the child.
Form C63: Apply for a declaration about whether a named person is the parent of another named person.
Form C64: Application for declaration of legitimacy or legitimation under section 56(1)(b) and (2) of the Family Law Act 1986.
Form C67: Application under the Child Abduction and Custody Act 1985 or Article 11 of Council Regulation (EC) 2201/2003.
Form C69: Application for registration, recognition or non-recognition of a judgment under Council Regulation (EC) 2201/2003 or the 1996 Hague Convention.

FORMS FOR APPEAL OF LOWER COURT CHILD ARRANGEMENT ORDERS

A father who believes an order for Child Arrangements under the CA 1989 is not only wrong, but legally incompetent or incorrect, for example, that it breaks a law or the court case did not follow the rules of court in some important respect, can apply for the order to be changed, set-aside or for the court case to be re-run. This process also gives the other party in the original court case a chance to take part as well, defending the original order. The two forms that start this appeals process are:

Form FP161: Appellant's notice (For use in appeals to the Family Division of the High Court).
Form FP162: Respondent's notice (For use in appeals in the Family Division of the High Court).

APPENDIX III
Exemplar- court document header

Name of person making statement

FIRST STATEMENT

EXHIBITS X1, X2..

dd/mm/yyyy

IN THE Town **FAMILY COURT**
CASE NUMBER:

IN THE MATTER OF Child's name & Date of Birth

AND IN THE MATTER OF THE CHILDREN ACT 1989

B E T W E E N:

Applicant

-and-

Respondent

1st WITNESS STATEMENT OF THE APPLICANT

I, name of applicant of 83 Sodmore Street …., make this statement pursuant to the order dated dd/mm/yyy and in response to other party's name and in support of my application for a Section 8 Child Arrangements Order. I am the father of the child xxx. All matters contained in this statement are within my own knowledge unless otherwise stated.

1. Lorem ipsum dolor sit amet, consectetuer adipiscing elit. Maecenas porttitor congue massa. Fusce posuere, magna sed pulvinar ultricies, purus lectus malesuada libero, sit amet commodo magna eros quis urna. Nunc viverra imperdiet enim. Fusce est.

2. Lorem ipsum dolor sit amet, consectetuer adipiscing elit. Maecenas

APPENDIX IV

List of ULRs for websites and online downloads, mentioned in the text. These are also given in Quick Response (QR) codes for mobile phones or tablets. Android users need to download a QR Scanner App. IPhones and iPads have this feature inbuilt.

1. WEBSITES FOR HELP MAKING OUT-OF-COURT AGREEMENTS

Section 2.1 of Family Court Practice Direction 12B. Meant to help identify mediators or information on how to do a DIY out-of-court agreement. This includes **links to MIAM mediators**.
https://www.justice.gov.uk/courts/procedure-rules/family/practice_directions/pd_part_12b#para2.1

Website listing people accredited to do **Family Law Arbitration**.

http://ifla.org.uk/

2. LINKS TO DOWNLOADABLE FORMS

Court & Tribunal Form Finder site. If you want to find any form shown in Appendix II, or any of the other court forms not highlighted there, you can find them on this Government website. For Private Law Family Court forms alone, click on 'Children Act Forms'. For forms to do with injunctions, click on 'Family Law Forms'.

https://www.gov.uk/government/collections/court-and-tribunal-forms

Form 120. Witness Statement form, an optional form for a Family Court cases.
https://www.gov.uk/government/publications/form-c120-witness-statement-template-child-arrangements-parental-dispute

3. LINKS TO ONLINE PUBLISHED LEGISLATION

Family Court Practice Direction 12B – describing the court rules for a Child Arrangement Programme (CAP) court case.

https://www.justice.gov.uk/courts/procedure-rules/family/practice_directions/pd_part_12b

Children Act 1989 (CA 1989) NB: Changes to this act have been made in subsequent Law Acts such as in 2014. These additional Acts together with the original CA 1989 are still collectively called by lawyers the CA 1989. However, online they will be listed seperately.

http://www.legislation.gov.uk/ukpga/1989/41/contents

Bailii Website for searching case histories.

http://www.bailii.org/

Rules on how to prepare a Court Bundle.

https://www.justice.gov.uk/courts/procedure-rules/family/practice_directions/pd_part_27a

4. LINKS TO LEGAL AID TOOLS

List of **types of abuses that qualify you to make a claim for Legal Aid.**
https://assets.publishing.service.gov.uk/government/uploads/system/uploads/attachment_data/file/509614/domestic-violence-child-abuse-offences.pdf

Government online tool for **checking eligibility for Legal Aid** funding.

https://www.gov.uk/check-legal-aid

FNF-Both Parents Matter weblink to an article **for fathers on how to obtain Legal Aid using the CDA mechanism**.

https://www.fnf-bpm.org.uk/article/legal_aid-253/index.html#.Xs-9er73JPY

5. OTHER HELP WEBSITES

The Personal Support Unit for Courts. Free in-person asistance by volunteers, for those new to the courts.

https://www.supportthroughcourt.org/

APPENDIX V
List of headings for a Section 7 CAFCASS Report

A. Nature of proceedings.

B. Matters at Issue.

C. Family composition and child(ren)'s current place of residence.

D. Enquiries made, and of whom.

E. Relevant background information.
   i. History of court proceedings.
   ii. A brief history of the relationship between the parties.
   iii. The history of Children's Services involvement and other agency interventions.
   iv. Existing arrangements for residence and contact.
   v. Significant other people.
   vi. Relevant issues such as domestic violence, child abduction, disruption during contact, allegations of abuse, health, education, criminal conviction details etc.

F. Applicant's details.
   i. A brief summary of each of current circumstances/relationships and views on the application.
   ii. Context of the dispute (as it affects the children and of the steps taken during the enquiry to help reduce and manage conflict/tensions).
   iii. Attitude to and reason for application/opposition. Attitude to children's needs/wishes if not covered in the Welfare Checklist.
   iv. Proposals and specific concerns/allegations with any evidence.
   v. Use of assessment tools (e.g. parenting plan) if appropriate.
   vi. Response to other party's allegations

G. Respondent's details – same as above.

H. Information on the Children.
   i. Description of the family relationships and attachments.
   ii. Observations of children and relationships with parents.
   iii. Information about the child's domestic situation, schooling, ethnicity, religion, language, disabilities and any special needs.
   iv. Whereabouts of interested parties in relation to the children.

I. Welfare Checklist.
   i. The ascertainable wishes and feelings of the children concerned.
   ii. Their physical, emotional and educational needs.
   iii. The likely effect of any change of circumstances.
   iv. Their age, sex, background and any characteristics which the Ccourt considers relevant.
   v. Any harm which they have suffered or are at risk of suffering.
   vi. The court's powers under the CA 1989.

J. Assessment.

K. Recommendations.

Further Reading & Media

Representing Yourself in a Scottish Family Court - A guide for Party Litigants in child contact and residence cases – by FNF Scotland, March 2014. This is a highly useful 50-page self-help guide for LiPs in Family Courts North of the boarder. Produced by a modest team of helpers it is only available as a file-download from FNF Scotland's website. Scan the QR code opposite, or type in the ULR address below for a direct link to this work.

http://static1.1.sqspcdn.com/static/f/861186/24542841/1395073043610/Represen tng+Yourself+in+a+Scottish+Family+Court.pdf?token=BwreMowo6MU%2BANX TU0TM%2FMcgfBc%3D

The Red Pill is an American documentary by the independent filmmaker and ex-feminist Cassie Jaye. The film explores Men's Rights Movements as Jaye spends a year filming 44 leaders and followers of these movements. The title refers to a scene in the film *The Matrix*, where the protagonist is offered the choice of a red pill, representing truth and self-knowledge, or a blue pill representing a return to blissful ignorance. By analogy, the film brings awareness of the contrast between men's and Fathers' Rights Groups and modern society's gynocentric attitudes.

Sexual Impolitics, heresies on sex, gender and feminism. Available on Amazon as an eBook. Neil Lyndon is an ex-journalist, and now a self-publisher. In this rewrite of his earlier work, Lyndon attempts to demolish the notion that we live in a patriarchal society and to show that change for women has taken place primarily as a result of advances in contraceptive and abortion technologies. Lyndon argues that mass-produced condoms, Dutch caps and contraceptive pills were the cause of female emancipation rather than the Pankhursts. Men as a whole, he argues, did not oppose egalitarian progress for women, which was frequently initiated, encouraged and promoted by men.

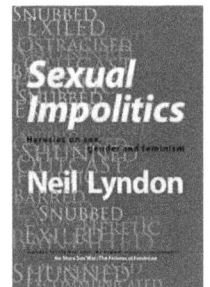

The illustrated Empathy Gap by William Collins. Collins (not his real name) has amassed an impressive collection of information, reports and statistics on sexual-inequality and discrimination against men, on a broad range of topics. A lot this store of facts he uses in a series of online works, many linked to a fringe political movement for Men's Rights. Although he is perhaps best known for his website and his talks, he has lately released a Vanity Press paperback with the same name as his website.

View his work online at www.empathygap.uk. For the book: **ISBN: 978-0-9571688-8-6**

Other books by Manhandle Press

ESCAPE FROM THE GIBBON SANCTUARY

"... there comes a point when you realize that ... society is arbitrary. It rewards good behavior and it rewards bad behavior, and sometimes even if you are good, it nevertheless pokes you in the eye," said the Thai monk to Michael, a journalist still in his twenties and still looking for answers.

Peter already understood a lot about the world when he jumped on a flight to Manila. Nevertheless, far from the normality of home, he became entangled in a classic fantasy, as if he knew nothing. Had he made a mistake? Where do you draw the line? In the genre of the books: Coming up for Air, Burmese Days, Lolita and Saint Jack. Escape from the Gibbon Sanctuary, is set in 1990's Philippines at a time when smoking was still allowed on airplanes and the Spice Girls were first enjoying their hit with Wannabe. Told mostly through the eyes of the main character, this book takes the reader on a journey of self-discovery, through a tsunami and shanty towns, from Luzon to Boracay.

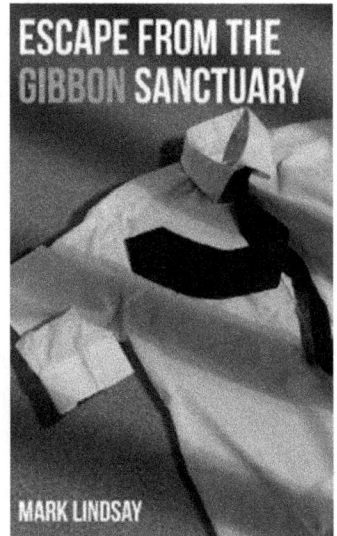

ISBN: 978-0-9926682-1-8

TRAVELS IN THE MIDDLE LAND

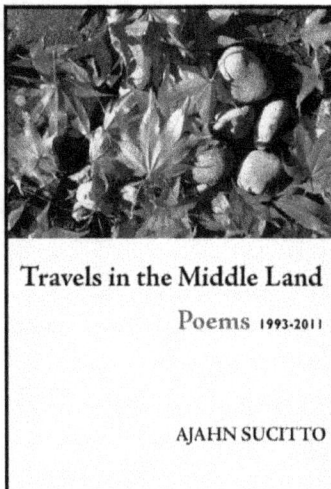

Theravada monks of the forest tradition remove themselves from all attachments: to place, to belongings and, most importantly to states of mind. They spend much of their time isolated in forests, but they also wander from place to place to both support their own practice and let their example be known. In this book the places the author travels through are both physical and spiritual; the poems present them as blending. In the author's view, living in the present moment means that where a body and mind meet this very earth, there is a place of awakening, mystery and beauty.

The publisher warrants that they will make no profit from the sale of this work. Any cover charge is solely as a result of the printing and/or distribution companies' mode of operation.

ISBN: 978-0-9926685-2-5

Notes

Notes